Anne Hutchinson:

Troubler of the Puritan Zion

ANNE HUTCHINSON:
Troubler of the Puritan Zion

edited by
FRANCIS J. BREMER
Department of History
Millersville State College

ROBERT E. KRIEGER PUBLISHING COMPANY
HUNTINGTON, NEW YORK
1981

Original Edition 1981

Printed and Published by
ROBERT E. KRIEGER PUBLISHING COMPANY, INC.
645 NEW YORK AVENUE
HUNTINGTON, NEW YORK 11743

·F 67
, H 9 2
A 5 6

Library of Congress Cataloging in Publication Data

Main entry under title:
  Anne Hutchinson: Troubler of the Puritan Zion

  Bibliography: p.
  1. Hutchinson, Anne Marbury, 1591-1643—Addresses,
essays, lectures.   2. Antinomianism—Addresses, essays,
lectures.   3. Religious liberty—Massachusetts—Addresses,
essays, lectures.   4. Women—Massachusetts—History—
Addresses, essays, lectures.   5. Massachusetts—Biography
—Addresses, essays, lectures.   6. Social reformers—Massachusetts—Biography—Addresses, essays, lectures.
I. Bremer, Francis J.
[F67.H92A56 1980]   273'.6'0924 [B]   80-13218
ISBN 0-89874-063-0

for

KRISTIN

whose interest in "true" stories
offers hope that history has value
for yet another generation

ACKNOWLEDGEMENTS

The author and publisher acknowledge with thanks the utilization of the following material:

1. Emery Battis, "Thine Eyes Shall See Thy Teachers", *Saints and Sectaries* Chapel Hill, 1962, pp.50-56.
2. Emery Battis, "A Diagnosis of Mrs. Hutchinson's Behavior in Terms of Menopausal Symptoms", *Saints and Sectaries* Chapel Hill, 1962, p. 346.
3. David Hall "Introduction" Reprinted from *The Antinomian Controversy, 1636-1638: A Documentary History* (Middletown, CT 1968), pp. 11-20 Copyright © Wesleyan University. Reprinted by permission of Wesleyan University Press.
4. William K.B. Stoever, "Nature, Grace and John Cotton: The Theological Dimensions in the New England Antinomian Controversy", *Church History*, 44, (1975) pgs. 22-33 abridged. Copyright © 1975 The American Society of Church History.
5. Jesper Rosenmeier, "New England's Perfection: The Image of Adam and the Image of Christ in the Antinomian Crises, 1634 to 1638", *William and Mary Quarterly*, 3rd series, XXVII (1970) pgs. 435-459 abridged.
6. Edmund S. Morgan, "The Case Against Anne Hutchinson", *New England Quarterly* X (1937) abridged.
7. Richard B. Morris, "Jezebel Before the Judges", in *Fair Trial* (New York, 1952) pp. 3-32.
8. Anne F. Withington and Jack Schwartz, "The Political Trial of Anne Hutchinson", *New England Quarterly*, LI (1978).
9. Kai Erikson, "The Antinomian Controversy", in Wayward Puritans: *A Study of the Sociology of Deviance* (New York, 1966), pp. 71-106.
10. Patricia Caldwell, "The Antinomian Language Controversy", *Harvard Theological Review* (1976) pp. 345-367 Copyright © 1977 by the President and Fellows of Harvard College.
11. Ben Barker-Benfield, "Anne Hutchinson and the Puritan Attitude Toward Women", *Feminist Studies*, Vol. 1, Number 2, (Fall 1972) pp. 65-96 by permission of the publisher FEMINIST STUDIES, Inc., c/o Women's Studies Program, University of Maryland, College Park, MD 20742.
12. Lyle Koehler, "The Case of the American Jezebels: Anne Hutchinson and Female Agitation during the Years of the Antinomian Turmoil, 1636-1640", *William and Mary Quarterly*, 3rd series, XXXI (1974), pp. 55-78 abridged Copyright © Lyle Koehler, the Director of Tutorial and Referral Services at the University of Cincinnati, author of A SEARCH FOR POWER: THE "WEAKER SEX" IN SEVENTEENTH-CENTURY NEW ENGLAND (University of Illinois Press, 1980).
13. Michael Colacurcio, "Footsteps of Anne Hutchinson: The Context of the Scarlett Letter", ELH, XXXIX (1972) pp. 459-494.
14. Mary Maples Dunn, "Saints and Sinners: Congregational & Quaker Women in the Early Colonial Period" AQ Vol. 30, No. 5, pp. 582-601, reprinted by permission of the *American Quarterly*, Copyright © 1979, Trustees of the University of Pennsylvania.

Contents

Introduction

The controversy that swirled around Anne Hutchinson in Massachusetts during the 1630s is one of those paradigmatic episodes in American history that seem to have an importance transcending the facts themselves. Like the Salem witchcraft hysteria, the siege of the Alamo, John Brown's raid on Harper's Ferry and similar moments, the clash between Mistress Hutchinson and the Massachusetts authorities has inherent drama and the spark of strong and colorful personalities while it illuminates in its glare the concerns, beliefs and realities of a particular culture at a particular time. From the first narratives written by those who sat in judgement on the Hutchinsonians to the historical monographs of today, those who have written about the controversy have perceived it as one which signalled to the world what the Puritan Commonwealth stood for and what it refused to tolerate. There is something in the record for those who are interested in Puritan theology—because the controversy was essentially a religious one—but there is also material for those who wish to know about Massachusetts culture, politics and law, and the status of colonial women. This anthology brings together the results of such searches by various historians, each with his or her particular insights into the past.

But who was this singular woman who posed what was perhaps the most dangerous challenge that the Massachusetts establishment was forced to cope with during their colony's first half-century? She was born in England in 1591, the second of the thirteen children of the Reverend Francis Marbury and his wife Bridget. Her father was an Anglican pastor with strong convictions and spirit whose calls for an "able clergy" involved him in recurrent clashes with his ecclesiastical superiors. He had twice been censured and imprisoned prior to settling in Alford, county Lancashire, where he met and wed Bridget Dryden. Domestic responsibilities did not temper his outspoken nature and he was deprived of his ministerial living shortly before the birth of Anne, his first daughter.

The Reverend Marbury continued to live in Alford, where Anne spent the first fifteen years of her life. Raised by a father with a strong commitment to learning, she not only received a better education than most girls of her time, but she became familiar with scripture and dogma as only the

1

daughter of a dedicated clergyman could have. Her father's strong personality left its mark, perhaps planting in the young girl the seeds of independence and the courage to challenge clerical authority which were to emerge in the mature woman.

In 1605 the family moved to London where once more Francis Marbury was allowed to exercise his ministry. For all his outspokenness he seemed free of the taint of Puritanism and that was sufficient for the Bishop of London, who tolerated Marbury's preaching until the pastor's death in 1611. One year later twenty-one year old William Hutchinson, an old friend from Alford, came south to London to wed Anne Marbury.

Willaim Hutchinson was a merchant on the rise. He and his new wife lived comfortably in Alford for twenty-two years, surrounded by a growing family. In all they had fifteen children, fourteen of them born while the couple was still in England. One son, William, died while still a youth. Two daughters, Susanna and Elizabeth, died in 1630 from the plague that swept the countryside that year. To have given birth to so many children was unusual, but not extraordinary. To have survived so many pregnancies required considerable physical and mental strength. The very real threat of death as a result of childbirth was an ever-present worry to all women of childbearing years.

While living with her husband in Alford, Anne found a substitute for the spiritual influence which her father had exerted over her early years. He was the Reverend John Cotton, a Puritan clergyman whose role in the Antinomian Controversy would be second only to Anne's. Cotton was a graduate of Emmanuel College, Cambridge University. He had been strongly influenced by the views of Richard Sibbes. Sibbes, and Cotton after him, represented the more mystical element in the Puritan movement. Placing less emphasis than their fellow clergymen on man's struggle to prepare himself for God's call, they stressed the immediacy and transforming character of the moment of religious conversion in which mortal man was infused with a divine grace. Cotton downplayed the role of works in man's relationship with God. He became one of the most distinguished of the Puritan clergy and his parish of St. Botolph's in Boston, Lincolnshire, was one of the centers of English Puritanism.

While attention naturally focuses on John Cotton as the guiding force in the mature Anne Hutchinson's spiritual life, it would be wrong to ignore the broader religious environment. Even nearer to the Hutchinson home than Boston was the town of Bilsby, whose young clergyman John Wheelwright married Anne's sister-in-law in 1630. Wheelwright preached a spiritual message similar to Cotton's and he became a second support and a frequent visitor in the Hutchinson household.

Attendance at services led by reformers such as Cotton and Wheelwright was not sufficient for many Puritan laymen and laywomen. In a church such as St. Botolph's they were forced to worship and receive the sacraments along with parishioners who shared neither their moral commitment nor their sense of religious rebirth. In his capacity as a clergyman of the Church of England a John Cotton could bend the rules set down by the episcopacy, but not consistently ignore them. These circumstances gave rise to the growth of conventicles—gatherings of those who had found grace and who came together with other "saints" to listen to repetitions of sermons and discuss them, to debate dark places in scripture, and to pray. Some of these private meetings were led by clergymen, others received their direction from the laity. All, of course, were frowned upon by the church hierarchy and even many of the Puritan clergy were ambivalent about them. While conventicles nurtured the embattled Puritan movement they also frequently gave a forum to lay preachers whose views were beyond the pale as far as most Puritan pastors were concerned. The beliefs held by the members of the various conventicles are difficult to discover. Some groups achieved a reputation for views more heretical than they actually held simply because deviants were expected to hold monstrous heresies. Numerous groups in Lincolnshire and nearby Cambridgeshire were suspected of anabaptist, familist, and other notorious opinions.

There is some evidence that women played a particularly active role in such assemblies, finding there an opportunity to speak out and exert the religious leadership denied them within the structure of the church. One such preacher of dubious doctrines was an unidentified "woman of Ely" whose activities were known to Anne Hutchinson. Anne seems to have been impressed with the evangelists's role if not with her views.

In 1633 John Cotton was forced from his living by the Anglican authorities and departed for New England and the ministry of the first church of the new Boston in Massachusetts. A year earlier Wheelwright had been suspended from his parish. Anne, whose mystical leanings had on previous occasions resulted in her having private revelations from God, now believed that the Spirit instructed her to follow Cotton to America. She was not the only person in England who felt such urgings and there is no reason to believe that her family was anything but impressed by this evidence of divine providence touching their lives. Certainly they accepted what Anne told them was God's will.

In September of 1634 the Hutchinson family arrived in Boston. The community, the center of the Bay colony, was still young enough to offer a skillful merchant like William ample opportunity to prosper. Starting in the cloth trade, he soon broadened his activities to include land purchases and various other investments. At a time when the colony's citizens eyed many merchants suspiciously, William Hutchinson earned their trust and was elected a town selectman and a deputy to the General Court, the colony's legislative assembly.

Anne likewise seemed to fit into her new home with minimal difficulty. She displayed an outgoing personality and a concern for the sick, devoting many hours serving those in need. While visiting her charges and entertaining friends she undoubtedly indulged the appetite for religious discourse which she had developed in conversations with her father. Perhaps she and her new friends also expressed a longing for the special intimacy that had existed in the private religious meetings which they had attended in England. Secret conventicles were unnecessary in New England, where the Puritans themselves were the establishment, but the appetite for them had not died. And so Mistress Hutchinson began to host twice weekly meetings in her home where those who came listened to restatements of Cotton's sermons and turned to Anne for explanations and elaborations of the clergyman's message.

The growth of Anne's following was probably attributable to a number of factors. One was the seemingly insatiable longing which the early New Englanders had for religious stimulation. Special lecture days on which the faithful gathered in their churches to hear sermons were called so frequently in the 1630s that the magistrates complained about the amount of important work being neglected. In the first church of Boston the preaching of John Cotton sparked an intense religious revival in 1633. Many citizens experienced the transforming nature of conversion. It was in such an environment that the meetings in the Hutchinson home began.

As time went on Anne began to devote more of her effort to an explication of her own views. Though her starting point was Cotton's emphasis on the force of grace, she preached that saving grace involved the actual indwelling of the divine and that an intuition of that spirit and not good works was the only valid proof of one's election. How far this represented Cotton's views and how far it was new doctrine was to become one of the major points of the controversy. In any case Anne attracted many of the leading citizens of the community, including the newly arrived Henry Vane. Vane was the son of one of the king's privy councillors and had been elected governor of Massachusetts. Some leading merchants and craftsmen who felt that their economic advancement was inhibited by the community's commitment to individual self-restraint found attractive the Hutchinsonian disassociation of the state of a man's soul and his outward behavior.

Anne Hutchinson and her followers were soon accused of antinomianism and familism, the former charge giving a name to the resultant controversy. There were opinions feared by most seventeenth century Englishmen and it is understandable that the Puritan leaders would seek to brand their opponents with such labels. Antinomianism was the belief that since the saints are under the law of grace the moral law was not binding on them. This raised the spectre of men and women seeking to justify all sorts of deviations from the norms of the church and the state. It is not surprising that those accused of antinomianism were also suspected of being familists, presumed disciples of the Family of Love, a sixteenth century sect which was incorrectly believed to have indulged in free love. The followers of Anne Hutchinson were certainly not familists in that sense and there is some question as to whether they were truly antinomians.

Clashes began to occur in 1635 with the return to the Boston church of

John Wilson, Cotton's senior colleague who had been back in England settling his affairs. Wilson's sermons stressed the need for preparation and the value of sanctification as evidence of salvation. Anne and her followers saw no difference between what Wilson preached and the hated Covenant of Works, the notion that man could earn his eternal reward. The Hutchinsonians soon found that Wilson's views were shared by all the clergy in the Bay except Cotton and Anne's newly arrived brother-in-law John Wheelwright. Criticism of Wilson broadened to include virtually the entire clerical establishment. What was at stake was the nature of the Puritans' holy experiment. But this wasn't all. Anne Hutchinson was no more tolerant than the ministers she mistrusted. The residents of the colony believed that there was only one true faith. They differed over what the nature of that faith was but they shared the conviction that the godly had an obligation to uphold the truth and suppress error. If it soon became ovbious that the orthodox majority would not tolerate the Hutchinsonians, it first became evident that the Hutchinsonians had no intention of tolerating advocates of what they viewed as the Covenant of Works. Anne and her allies disrupted Wilson's sermons and generated divisive debates in the Boston church. When troops were called out to meet the military threat of the Pequot tribe, members of Anne's faction refused to serve because Wilson was the expedition's chaplain.

The men who had led the great migration to New England believed themselves called by God to create in the American wilderness a model society, a "City on a Hill" which would transform England and the world by its Puritan example. Their understanding of their mission required a clear definition of orthodoxy and an insistence that all subscribe to that formula. Leaders of the orthodox party began to move against the Hutchinsonians in 1637. In March the General Court condemned as seditious a sermon preached by John Wheelwright. In that year's elections John Winthrop, the most distinguished political leader of the first generation, was returned to the governor's office. The departure for England of the defeated Henry Vane deprived the Hutchinsonians of their foremost champion.

In September of 1637 an assembly of representatives from the region's churches issued a condemnation of religious errors said to be circulating in the colony. The synod's statement successfully defined the limits of Massachusetts orthodoxy; to what extent the errors condemned were an accurate compendium of views actually held by the dissidents is still difficult to assess. Even in calmer moments the orthodox tended to read into dissenting movements all sorts of extreme opinions which the actual dissenters may not have subscribed to. It was simply assumed that certain heresies were to be found in all deviant groups.

The General Court, presided over by Winthrop, called John Wheelwright to account in November of 1637. He was convicted of sedition and contempt and sentenced to banishment. Prominent Boston supporters of Wheelwright and Hutchinson were called before the Court for signing a petition in defense of the clergyman. For their seditious behavior some were banished and others disenfranchised. Finally it was the turn of Anne Hutchinson. The confrontation was one of the most dramatic events of early American history. Her claim of having received direct revelations from God climaxed the trial and sealed her fate. She was sentenced to banishment and remanded to custody until the Spring, when the sentence would be carried out. In March of 1638 she was tried for heresy in the Boston church and formally excommunicated. Cotton, who for a time in 1637 had been in danger of going the way of Wheelwright and Hutchinson, clarified his position and made peace with the orthodox. Thomas Shepard and other ministers had doubts about Cotton for a number of years. They weren't sure if his clarification represented a true revulsion from what he had finally realized Anne was saying or whether it was an expedient rejection of views he had once held. Historians still puzzle over the answer to that question.

The Antinomian Controversy came to a close with Anne Hutchinson's departure from the Bay, but the story of Anne went on. While John Wheelwright journeyed north to a New Hampshire exile, most of the Antinomians sought new homes on Narraganset Bay. William Hutchinson, William Coddington and over eighty other men and their families obtained title to Aquidneck Island from the Narraganset Indians. On the north end of the island they built a town called Pocasset, later renamed Portsmouth. Coddington, who had been a magistrate and treasurer of the Massachusetts Bay Colony, assumed leadership of the new settlement.

As time went on most of the inhabitants of Aquidneck came to worship in a manner that bore no striking difference from that of their former neighbors in Massachusetts. Some, however, continued to explore the paths of religious experimentation upon which they had first embarked in the Hutchinsons' front room. Lay prophesying had traditionally been part of the Puritan movement but now zealots were speaking out under the belief that the Spirit directly inspired them. The arrival of Samuel Gorton, another of New England's Puritan radicals, contributed to the spread of this mysticism. The community soon began to divide in disputes over the appropriatness of newly advanced ideas and practices.

Political divisions also troubled Portsmouth. The original settlers had drawn up a social compact pledging themselves to live under the kingship of Christ and the law of the Bible. Coddington was chosen to rule as an Old Testament style "judge". His dominance of the community was irksome to many, perhaps to Anne Hutchinson, who faded from her former prominence during her early years in Portsmouth. Others challenged the town's land policy. Tensions continued to build until Coddington and some of his supporters were forced out and moved to the southern end of Aquidneck where they established the town of Newport.

The government of Portsmouth was reorganized under English rather than Biblical law and William Hutchinson was elected judge. Soon an accomodation was reached with the Newport settlement. When Gorton con-

tinued to exert a disruptive influence he was banished. Most of the Hutchinsonians were settling into the type of mystical pietism that in a few decades
would become characteristic of the Society of Friends, the Quakers. In fact,
when the first English Quaker missionaries reached Rhode Island they would
bring former Antinomians such as Mary Dyer into the Friends. But Anne
Hutchinson would not be there to participate in or to observe the final
transformation of the movement she had begun.

William Hutchinson died in 1642. With the death of her husband Anne's
interest in the contentions of Rhode Island paled and she moved once again.
Accompanied by her six youngest children she journeyed to the Dutch
colony of New Netherland, settling along what is now called the Hutchinson
River in the Bronx. There, a year later, all of the family except the youngest
daughter were killed in an Indian raid.

At one time it was fashionable to label Anne Hutchinson a pioneer of
religious liberty. Today no historian would give her that accolade, though
many would point out that in her steadfast advocacy of her views she
contributed to the growth of a pluralistic society which eventually made
toleration imperative. But if she is no longer appreciated for the wrong
reason, she is better understood for the woman she actually was. Articles
selected for this collection describe her personality, her religious views, and
her accomplishment in transcending the roles ascribed to women in her time.
Other articles examine the controversy she provoked, both as a means of
appreciating her impact and as a means of coming to a clearer understanding
of the society of which she was a part, but which ultimately rejected her.
From those essays the reader may gain an appreciation of why the people
of the Bay became so stirred up over issues which seem terribly abstract and
unimportant to most Americans today. The articles also reveal some of the
problems that afflict any society in the process of defining itself. And some
of the issues raised—the role of women, the limits of dissent, political trials—
will seem as contemporary as today's newspapers.

There is one theme that deserves special comment. At a time when the
struggle for women's rights is of widespread concern, it is easy to exagerate
the role of famous women and to read self-conscious feminism into an age
when such notions had no meaning. Some of the following essays do perhaps
err in that direction in their authors' concern to explain the sexual aspects of
the controversy. But the existence of such a dimension cannot be denied.
Whoever reads the surviving documents on the controversy or the range
of secondary literature that deals with it must conclude that the fact that
this dissenter was a woman made a difference. The clergy were unaccustomed
to debating a woman; the magistrates were chagrined to have such a challenge posed to their authority. To all of the authorities Anne Hutchinson
represented not only a challenge to religious order and to political order,
but to the very order of nature. Whatever the motivation for her dissent, no
one expected a challenge from a woman. No one in the Bay had really

believed that a woman was capable of such a challenge. Anne Hutchinson shattered that illusion.

All of the articles in this collection have been abridged and footnotes have been deleted. Readers whose interest is captured by the anthology and who have the opportunity to do so are urged to benefit from the authors' full elaboration of their points in the original articles and books.

There are a number of individuals whose assistance I would like to acknowledge. To undertake any work of scholarship one requires encouragement and support. It is more than a *pro forma* tip of the cap when I express my gratitude to my colleagues in the Millersville History Department for the interest they have shown in this project. In a different fashion I have been sustained in this and other works by my parents, my wife and my children. An interest in the personality of Anne Hutchinson seemed a natural outgrowth of life with four such unique and strong female personalities as Barbara and our three daughters—Heather, Kristin and Megan.

There is one final debt that deserves acknowledgement. If Anne Hutchinson was able to speak to us she would wish us to remember her husband Bill. Without his constant love and understanding, his willingness to twice uproot his business and leave his friends, his generosity in putting up with all the meetings in his home, and his undying belief in her views and the voices she heard, this anthology would not have been possible.

Anne Hutchinson:
The Woman Who Heard Voices

In *Saints and Sectaries* Emery Battis uses the concepts and methods of a variety of social sciences to seek an understanding of why Anne Hutchinson believed and behaved as she did and why she attracted support from the particular segments of the community that rallied to her banner. In this selection from that study Battis speculates on the probable psychological profile of Mistress Hutchinson. In addition to seeking the general causes of the mystic tendencies which she manifested, Battis offers an explanation of the specific events that he believes initiated her experiences.

EMERY BATTIS

"Thine Eyes Shall See Thy Teachers"

The fluent revelations of Anne Hutchinson, much as they may have bespoken the pattern of the Godhead, were even more revelatory of her own complex psychological structure. Like her colleagues in this terrestrial enterprise, she was impelled to invoke the unknowable divine in terms that satisfied not only her cultural preconceptions but the modifying force of her emotional needs. Her religious professions, like theirs, often represented a rationalization of motives known only to her subconscious.

Close scrutiny of Mrs. Hutchinson's career reveals a pattern of psychological needs which were expressed in the concurrent and congruent roles of mystic, Antinomian, and religious agitator. It is not surprising that her psychological imbalance should resolve itself in religious formulas. She was raised and educated in a clerical household, and the cultural environment in which she moved was predominantly religious.

During her later years Mrs. Hutchinson appears to have suffered a dread of isolation and an exaggerated craving for moral support, a form of anxiety

11

generally attributable to the lack of mental direction from a source where it is normally expected. Students in the field of religious psychology cite many instances of women who have been tormented by fixed ideas and hysterical manifestations because their husbands have failed to guide their mental life. They engage in an obsessive search for a substitute mental director, and until he is found they suffer a profound horror of isolation. When a satisfactory director is located, the subject becomes almost entirely dependent upon his guidance and support; in his presence insecurity and uneasiness are dispelled, and problems are approached with renewed assurance. With a person of strong religious bent, such an influence could be exerted by a confessor or pastor or—given the proper set of stimuli—even the Deity. In union with a loving God the mystic seeks to attain peace, affection, self-assurance, and mental direction. "To realize the presence of the God of Love is the Mystic's method of securing the satisfaction of his essential wants."

It has been observed that William Hutchinson seems to have lacked the power to provide adequate support and direction for his wife. The absence of this guidance, sharply felt after the firm influence of her father, apparently compelled Mrs. Hutchinson to turn elsewhere for affective support. In her extremely active social life she found the affection that enhanced her self-esteem. Mrs. Hutchinson was notably gregarious and her nusing activities brought ample rewards in gratitude and esteem. Also she suffered from a compulsion to verbalize her most errant thoughts, another unconscious device for the attainment of notice and approval.

More important, however, was her search for a substitute mental director.

At first she was drawn to John Cotton, in whom she found a suitable symbol of authority who fulfilled the directional function without inhibiting her own expressiveness or spontaneity. Later she was to form a similar attachment to Henry Vane, a young aristocrat who was for a time her neighbor in Massachusetts. But even more to the point was her implicit reliance upon the elaborately detailed directions which she professed to receive from God. She claimed that her spiritual communion yielded revelations "as trew as the Scriptures" and professed that "she had never had any great thing done about her but it was revealed to her beforehand." Here was a director for her mind with a vengeance! As a matter of fact, among authorities on the subject and even among the mystics themselves, claims of exterior visions and prophetic revelations such as Anne Hutchinson came to profess are not generally regarded as trustworthy evidence of union with the Divine Spirit. The extremity of Mrs. Hutchinson's claims may have been the result of a pressing need for guidance and moral support.*

---

*Psycological investigation has disclosed that a strong egoism is one of the basic roots of mystical behavior. Leuba asserts that the mystics are "determined not only to be worthwhile, but to be recognized as such. . . . Their light shall not shine under a bushel." This tendency to self-affirmation is related to the basic frustration suffered in the absence of adequate mental direction. When the love relationship encounters an obstacle such as this, the libido is effectively blocked and is obliged to withdraw from its outward movement and settle back upon the ego, resulting in a strong tendency toward narcissism. The consequent insecurity must be relieved and the individual requires constant evidence of his self-importance. Persistent efforts are made to attract and hold attention. Approval of one's actions is essential and the capacity to arouse the emotional response of the public in token of such approvel assumes primary importance. Leuba has observed this reaction in varying degrees in such diverse personalities as Francis of Assisi, Ignatius Loyola, and Saint Theresa. None of the mystics enjoyed a completely normal married life, most of them were consumed with a desire to shine, and many, in order to do so, laid dispropor-

There remains the possibility that Mrs Hutchinson's mystical experience was initiated by more explicit and immediate needs than those cited; that a specific catalytic agent triggered the tensions created by these needs and directed them toward this particular solution. It seems not improbable that the deaths of her children provided a major impulse toward such a psychological expression. Not only would the emotional shock attending this double tragedy have been in itself traumatic, but the event would have been subject to interpretations that must have imposed a severe mental strain on the distraught mother. These children were undoubtedly under her care during their final illness. However much she may have sought to console herself with the belief that this was God's will, Mrs. Hutchinson could hardly have escaped the feeling that her own inadequacy was at least in part responsible for their deaths. She was a person who placed excessive demands on herself and was intent on the preservation of a favorable self-image; therefore, it would have been essential to her emotional quiet to minimize this hideous burden of responsibility or convert it to more favorable terms.

The situation was further complicated by the ambivalent interpretation the Puritans imposed upon such events. Bereaved persons who were fully confident of the innocence of the deceased and of their own state of grace could profess satisfaction that their loved ones had ascended to a just and enviable reward. But for those whose election was held uncertain, by themselves or by the community, a tragedy of these proportions was generally construed to be a clear manifestation of God's wrath. From whatever perspective the event is viewed, it gives the appearance of a traumatic experience, the meaning of which Mrs. Hutchinson was forced to convert to more reassuring terms. Wracked with unbearable doubt, the unhappy woman was in all probability driven forward on a restless and compulsive quest for certainty.

There is no way of knowing that Mrs. Hutchinson's initial mystical experiences occurred at this precise moment in her career, but it is known that they assumed a curiously delusional quality that might well fit these circumstances, and it would seem that the traumatic impact of this tragedy was adequate to their excitation. Her great personal need at this juncture would have been to organize a frame of reference within which she might reaffirm her self-esteem. Given the fact of her religious orientation, with its harsh emphasis on the correlation of human conduct and divine retribution, it would have seemed necessary that she obtain an assurance of God's love and support that transcended all considerations of guilt and punishment, or of effort and reward. Very often when an individual who is the victim of his own excessive demands persecutes himself for an act conflicting with his ideals and expectations, he may conclude that others similarly blame him. Incapable of flexible adjustment to the strains imposed by the situation, he is impelled to ascribe imagined attitudes and functions to their persons. He formulates "hypothetical relationships between himself and others and organizes them into a pseudo-community." The pressure of self-esteem produces a convulsive attempt at exculpation and compensation for his feeling of guilt and inferi-

---

tionately high value on their ability to play upon the emotions of the public. It is noteworthy that Harold Lasswell has found similar impulses operating under the same conditions in the lives of the political agitators he has studied. Leuba, *Psychology of Religious Mysticism*, 121; Harold Lasswell, *Psychopathology and Politics* (Chicago, 1930), 124 ff.

ority, and a balancing delusion may be generated—one providing a sense of justification and even grandiosity. It seems possible that Mrs. Hutchinson, in this critical moment, may have created such a pseudo-community of imagined relationships to account for her dilemma: on the one hand the legalists, who presumably condemned her for her shortcomings, and on the other, the Deity, who accepted her despite the faults of which she felt secretly guilty. It has already been observed that her mystical locutions implied an intimate relationship with God superseding all legal conditions. She was assured that God would unalterably support her, and that her presumed persecutors—those who insisted on the legal correlation of conduct and retribution—would be forever cast down. It was indeed a "most desperate enthusiasm."

Succeeding developments may serve to confirm and expand this thesis. During the months following her tragic loss, Mrs. Hutchinson was succored by a physiological reinforcement of no slight value. During her hour of greatest need, when the loss of her children must have incurred a subsidence of self-affirmation, she became pregnant once again. The physiological adjustment subsequent to pregnancy resulted in an exaltation that increased or possibly even initiated a conviction of union with God transcending all legal considerations. In the lives of many of the mystics a marked periodicty has been frequently observed. It has been noted among female mystics that oscillations traceable to physiological causes are often the result of the exaltation accompanying pregnancy. It was not by coincidence that hysteria derived its name from the uterine function, and this exalted state frequently occurs among pregnant women, mystical or otherwise. Among

those of an extremely religious nature it is generally directed toward religious ends.

The pattern may be traced into Mrs. Hutchinson's future career. It was approximately during the period of a succeeding pregnancy, from July 1635 to March 1636, that she commenced her program of religious education and proselytizing in Massachusetts. The coincidence of pregnancies and religious exaltation did not escape the notice of her contemporaries. Several years later John Wheelwright spoke slightingly of the "strange fancies and erroneous tenets [which] possest her, especially during her confinement, where she might feel some effects too, from the quality of humours, together with the advantage the devil took of her condition attended with melancholy. Wheelwright may also have remembered similar experiences which he had seen her undergo when they were neighbors in Lincolnshire.

The mystic type is not necessarily Antinomian, but among Antinomians there has been a strong tendency to mysticism. The mystic way varies widely, the course followed depending as much on the prevailing conception of the nature of God as on the temperament of the individual. Antinomianism, however, often entailed a conception of the nature of God which was intrinsically mystical and its more prominent exponents were almost invariably mystics. Mrs. Hutchinson was was strongly inclined to mysticism; equally compelling motives seem to have led to her acceptance of Antinomianism.

The Puritan demand for rigorous self-examination greatly encouraged subjectivism, and the inadequate system of assurances laid down by Calvin aroused a cry for a surer knowledge of grace. Disregarding the attempts of theologians to straddle these delicate issues, Mrs. Hutchinson did not hesitate to travel the perilous road which stretched temptingly before her. Having chafed under the restrictions of the conventional theology she pursued the mild illuminism of John Cotton to its highly subjectivist conclusions and arrived on the far side of orthodoxy with a solution at once intellectually and emotionally satisfying.

The neurotic individual, seeking protection against weakness and helplessness, strives for power and constantly endeavors to offset the feeling of being insignificant, a tendency which generally results in an assertive and domineering attitude. In due course Mrs. Hutchinson would find broad scope for such an inclination in her activities as a religious teacher, malcontent, and dialectical opponent to the theologians of Massachusetts Bay. The Antinomian philosophy provided another such release. Theoretically, Antinomianism was a rejection of power by placing the human will in the hands of God, to be manipulated by Him as He saw fit. Practically, however it amounted to an assertion of unqualified personal power and autonomy. The individual became a law unto himself and reserved the right to make all decisions affecting his actions without reference to the needs of the community. Such a philosophy offered incalculable advantage to a nature that was constantly striving to prove its own value. Like the timid child who courts danger in order to draw attention and establish proof of his own courage, Mrs. Hutchinson wrenched herself free of narrowly defined social obligations and determined to steer her own course. The very radicalism of the doctrine commended itself by contributing to that singularity with which she sought to win attention and approval.

In the previous selection Battis sought to draw a general psychological profile of Anne Hutchinson. In this selection from one of the appendices of *Saints and Sectaries* Battis suggests a physiological cause behind some of Mrs. Hutchinson's behavior during the crisis. Battis does not believe that the stress of menopause gave rise to her beliefs but rather that her physical condition and the attendant stress could have shaped her expression of her views. As Battis points out, this hypothesis would also explain the reports that Mrs. Hutchinson gave birth to a "monster" in 1638. Such accounts were greeted eagerly by her enemies in Massachusetts, who viewed it as a sign from God that the woman who gave birth to such monstrous heresies would physically give birth to a monster.

EMERY BATTIS

"Mrs. Hutchinson's Behavior in Terms of Menopausal Symptoms"

Dr. John Clark's description in 1638 of Mrs. Hutchinson's delivery indicates that she had expelled an hydatidiform mole. Weighing this information, which is printed below, in conjunction with other available details of her medical history, Dr. Paul A. Younge of the Harvard Medical School has given a diagnosis which differs considerably from that conventionally accepted. Mrs. Hutchinson was not pregnant at the time of her trial in November, 1937, nor did she become pregnant for at least five months thereafter. At this time and during the ensuing winter months, she displayed the symptoms of the initial phase of menopause. A climacteric, attended by anemia and general anxiety, and exacerbated by the emotional shock she had undergone, would induce amenorrhea which would in turn lead her to suspect that she was again pregnant. In the following April, however, after rejoining her husband, she did become pregnant of the "menopausal baby" which aborted into an hydatidiform mole.

Mrs. Hutchinson's behavior during this crucial period can be explained largely in terms of menopausal symptoms. She was now forty-six years old and passing the limit of her reproductive activity. Women in this stage of life are especially susceptible to uterine growths of this nature. For twenty-five years Mrs. Hutchinson had undergone a continuous cycle of pregnancies, deliveries, and lactations, while simultaneously bearing the heavy cares of rearing a large family. A woman suffering the anemia attendant on such an obstetrical history, subjected at a critical physiological period to extreme mental stress would almost certainly experience severe menopausal symptoms including neurotic manifestations. Under these conditions such aspects of the delusional system which Mrs. Hutchinson may hitherto have entertained inwardly could have been forced into open expression.

The Religious Dispute

David Hall's *The Antinomian Controversy* is an extensive collection of contemporary accounts of the dispute that raged around Anne Hutchinson. In this selection from the introduction to that book Hall attempts to explain the Puritan concern with the way in which a man's soul was saved. He explains the background to the rise of "Antinomianism": the Puritan longing for grace, the religious revival touched off by John Cotton's preaching in 1633, and the subsequent religious depression of 1635-36. Anne Hutchinson offered an escape from the anxiety produced in the colony when the enthusiasm of 1633 had been replaced by a perceived decline in public piety.

DAVID HALL

"The Antinomian Controversy"

In the opinion of Charles Francis Adams, the Antinomian Controversy could not be properly appreciated if it were approached from a theological point of view. "As a rule," suggested Adams, "Theological controversies are ...among the most barren of the many barren fields of historical research; and the literature of which they were so fruitful may, so far as the reader of to-day is concerned, best be described by the single word impossible."

• • •

The following discussion addresses itself to the theological issues that Adams dismissed as "jargon." What were these issues? The most complete guide to them is the catalogue of "erroneous opinions" compiled at the synod of 1637. But this list is repetitious and indiscriminate; it also lumps together the opinions that emerged later on in the Controversy with those that circulated from the start. In searching for the root issues, this chronological distinction must be kept in mind, as well as the difference between the issues debated by the ministers and those injected into the Controversy by the more radical members of the Boston Church. In the beginning there were only two issues involved, according to Winthrop's reckoning: "1. That the person of the Holy Ghost dwells in a justified person. 2. That no sanctification can help to evidence to us our justification." The second of these statements figured as the major issue in the debate between John Cotton and his fellow ministers. Replying to the sixteen questions, Cotton answered "more largely and distinctly" to question thirteen, "Whether evidencing Justification by Sanctification, be a building my Justification on my Sanctification," it being, as he said, "exposed to greatest Agitation and Exception." According to Thomas Shepard, the "principall opinion & seed" of all the "monstrous opinions" condemned by the synod of 1637 was

> that a Christian should not take any euidence of gods speciall grace & loue toward him by the sight of any graces or conditionall euangelicall promises to fayth or sanctification; in way of ratiocination; (for this was ueidence & so a way of woorkes,) but it must be without the sight of any grace fayth holines or speciall change in himselfe. by immediat reuelation in an absulute promise. & because that the whole scriptures do giue such cleare plaine & notable euidences of favour to persons called & sanctifyed; hence they sayd that a second euidence might be taken from hence but no first euidence.

To this same issue, finally, Winthrop referred most often in his running account of the Controversy.

If we accept this testimony, the problem is then to understand why the relationship between justification and sanctification became so debatable in the 1630s. Part of the explanation lies in the background of the colonists. Like other English Puritans they assumed that everyone could know whether or not he was saved, or of the elect. The blunt question of the revivalist— "Brother, are you saved?—had its analogue in the evangelical preaching of the spiritual brotherhood, the fraternity of Puritan preachers in England. To help their listeners answer that question, the preachers wrote scores of books describing the process of conversion in which the elect came to know "experimentally" of their salvation. But no one who listened to the "painfull" sermons of the ministers could take his salvation for granted. The conversion experience was too variable, the "heart" of the sinner too shifting, for assurance to be complete. The result of the ministers' preaching was thus to arouse an acute anxiety in many of those who lacked assurance. The preachers could not resolve the problem by declaring that anxiety was inevitable. They had to provide some objective measure of grace, some outward sign of inner holiness. One such sign was sanctification, the daily course of living a godly life. Though the Puritans recognized that a hypocrite could simulate the life of righteousness, they reasoned that only the person whose heart had been transformed could sustain his obedience to the will of God Outward behaviour could therefore be taken as a sign—albeit a confusing one—of justification.

The colonists brought the problem of achieving assurance with them to New England, and in the new world a special set of circumstances made it more intense. One of these circumstances was the religious excitement that prevailed in Massachusetts during the early 1630s. While the colonists remained in England, they lived in the fear that the government would deprive them of their spiritual "food," the preaching of the spiritual brotherhood.

When Archibishop Laud made that year a reality by driving the Puritan preachers out of the Church, Puritan laymen risked their lives to found a new society in which evangelical preaching would be unrestrained. For the first time in their lives, these Puritans could indulge themselves in sermons, and there is ample evidence to suggest that they did so.

• • •

Out of this heightened longing for grace came a revival, a period of exaggerated piety. According to Roger Clap, who placed the beginning of this revival in 1633, it served as a means of relieving the anguish of dislocation:

> God's holy spirit in those days was pleased to accompany the word with such efficacy upon the hearts of many, that our hearts were taken off from old England and set upon heaven. The discourse not only of the aged, but of the youth also, was not, "How shall we go to England? ... but "How shall we go to heaven? Have I true grace wrought in my heart? Have I Christ or no?" O how did men and women, young and old, pray for grace, beg for Christ in those days. And it was not in vain. Many were converted, and others established in believing.

The Boston Church Records bear Clap out on the number of conversions. In the six months following John Cotton's admission to membership in September, 1633, sixty-three persons—or nearly half the number of members acquired during the previous three years—joined the church.

An increase in church membership was not the only consequence of the revival. At the time it occurred, the colonists were debating what standards of church membership they should adopt. The revival was to shape that debate in a crucial direction. The colonists wished to restrict the church to the godly, but they were not sure what terms to demand of prospective church members. By 1633, they had set up two requirements, soundness in doctrine and evidence of good behavior. Some of the ministers, among them John Cotton, wanted to go further by requiring candidates to testify before the church about their experience of conversion. Since the revival seemed to guarantee an abundance of conversions, the other ministers agreed, and in February, 1636, when Thomas Shepard formed a new church in Cambridge, the advice of the ministers present was "that such as were to join should make confession of their faith, and declare what work of grace the Lord had wrought in them; which accordingly they did."

But by 1636 the revival itself was over. For the first time in America, the ministers learned the lesson that the tide of grace soon ebbs. The reasons seemed clear. As the hardships of life in the new world diminished, the colonists were turning to other interests. Piety declined as the lure of prosperity grew stronger.

• • •

The collapse of the revival engendered a mood of acute religious anxiety. As Clap's account indicates, the revival and the new requirement for church membership were forcing everyone in the colony to ask himself, am I saved? In the aftermath of the revival many were not sure of the answer. How could they tell if they were saved or not? What evidence could they rely upon? How could they gain assurance of salvation and escape from anxiety about their spiritual estates? For one member of the Boston Church the answer to these questions was a desperate one.

"A woman of Boston congregation, having been in much trouble of mind about her spiritual estate, at length grew into utter desperation, and could not endure to hear of any comfort, etc., so as one day she took her little infant and threw it into a well, and then came into the house and said, now she was sure she should be damned, for she had drowned her child." Others, less desperate, found relief in cursing the ministers. Nowhere else in the world, remarked Shepard, had there been "such expectation to find the Lord," and for those who found Him not, the reaction against the ministers was intense: "They give in and therefore care not for . . . that food which they find nourisheth them not."

Thus the spiritual depression of 1635–1636 gave rise to an antiministerial attitude and an anxiety about the knowledge of God. All that was needed to turn these two ingredients into Antinomianism was the preaching of John Cotton. Cotton's sermons in Boston had touched off the revival of 1633, and in those he preached during the summer of 1636 he tried to get it going again. Piety had declined, declared Cotton, because the colonists had become too proud of New England's "Reformation" in manners. He reminded them that good behavior itself, or "walking in the wayes of God," as the various church covenants expressed it, was a "work" that any hypocrite could perform. Such "sanctification" could amount to no more than a "righteousness of ones own." In short, "Reformation is no assurance that God hath made an everlasting Covenant with us."

Against pride in "works" Cotton set the true measure of the saint. He was "Meek in Spirit & Merciful, and Mourning for Sin." He was overcome with a sense of his helplessness.

Now then, doth the Lord draw you to Christ, when you are broken in the sense of your own Sins, and of your own Righteousness? When you look at duties you are not able to do them, not able to hear or pray aright.

Rather than counting upon "duties" for assurance, the sinner must look to God.

If the Lord do thus draw you by his everlasting Arm, He will put a Spirit into you, that will cause you to wait for Christ, and to wait for Him until He doth shew Mercy upon you.

The person who waited for Christ, whose heart was "emptied of every thing besides," could be judged one of the elect, and hence be eligible for church membership: "You may safely receive him into your Church fellowship."

These themes reappeared in the conversation of Anne Hutchinson. Before the Controversy broke out, she had won Cotton's "loving and dear respect" for her efforts to overcome the spiritual deadness that he was also attacking. In her efforts to arouse the colonists "to seek for better establishment in Christ," Mrs. Hutchinson insisted that those who turned for comfort to the performance of "duties" were resting their assurance on "sandy foundations." To this extent her message was useful and legitimate. Even John Winthrop admitted that "the Doctrine of free justification lately taught here took me in as drowsy a condition, as I had been in (to my remembrance) these twenty yeares." But Anne Hutchinson did more than revive the colonists from their "drowsy" state. Taking up Cotton's warning against confidence in "works," she turned his denunciations of moralism into the specific charge that the other ministers in the colony were preaching a "Covenant of Works." By this term she meant that the ministers were letting people "thinke [themselves] to be saved, because they see some worke of Sanctification in them." More broadly, the term she used referred to the covenant God had made with Adam. As a man without sin, Adam could ensure his salvation by fulfilling the condition of perfect obedience, but after the Fall man's "works" no longer earned him any merit with God. In the new "covenant of grace" that God established with Abraham, the sole reasons for salvation were the Gospel of Christ and the free gift of grace.

Mrs. Hutchinson based her attack upon the "legall" preachers on the difference between these covenants. Between free grace and man's own righteousness she saw no connection, and therefore insisted on treating sanctification as a "work." From the radical disjunction between grace and "duties" flowed the rhetoric of the Antinomians:

> Here is a great stirre about graces and looking to hearts, but give mee Christ, I seeke not for graces, but for Christ, I seeke not for sanctification, but for Christ, tell not mee of meditation and duties, but tell mee of Christ.

On it was also based Anne Hutchinson's personal sense of communion with the Holy Spirit. Since her own piety rested upon an immediate awareness of the Spirit, she could deny that the ministry was needed as an intervening "means of grace" between God and man. And she could solve the problem of assurance by declaring that those who received the Spirit never had to doubt their estate again. In her system, and striving after "signs" of grace was a sure sign that grace had not been granted.

Anne Hutchinson brought most of these beliefs with her to New England, but they owed their currency in the colony to the spiritual depression of 1635–1636. The "Antinomians" in Massachusetts were primarily those who sought relief from their religious anxiety and support for their anger at the ministers. Antinomianism provided them with both. Yet there was an alternative route to assurance and one that, in the end, the majority of the colonists chose to follow. As described by Thomas Shepard in a series of sermons he began to preach in the summer of 1636, this route involved a ceaseless striving after grace by the saints and the unregenerate alike. In Shepard's view, the spiritual journey of the saint on earth became a constant growth in grace as he struggled to fulfill the commandd of God. Given this ceaseless struggle, the reasonn for the spiritual depression and the rise of Antinomianism was obvious. Antinomianism was simply a way for the "slothful" sinner to escape the demands of the law. Shepard had no patience with the argument that man was helpless; to the cry of the Antinomians, "We can do nothing, and why are we pressed to it?," he replied that God made room for man's own striving within the larger framework of the divine initiative. God and man worked together in the process of salvation: "Whereunto I also labor, striving according to his working, which worketh in me mightily" (Colossians 1.29). Since the grace of God made possible the efforts of the saint, Shepard argued that sanctification could be used as a valid sign of justification, or election. The same reasoning led him to his doctrine of assurance. Though anxiety was part of the "trial" of life in this world, the saint, said Shepard, could gain assurance from his own striving after righteousness. The answer to anxiety lay in constant activity.

The Controversy touched on other issues besides the relationship between justification and sanctification. One was the significance of "preparation" as a stage in the process of conversion. Did God demand that man prepare himself to receive grace? Did man's response to the "Law" have any saving efficacy? Cotton did not think so, but most of the ministers were "preparationists" to one degree or another. Another problem was determining the relationship between faith and grace. Like all Protestants, the colonists believed that salvation was the gift of a merciful God who only asked of man that he have faith. Could faith be considered the "condition" of the covenant of grace, the response man must make to the offer of the Gospel before God would grant him grace? Or was faith an aftereffect, a consequence of justification? Cotton held to the latter opinion, but his opponents believed that faith was the "active" instrument for receiving grace. Other issues besides these were involved in the ministers' debate, but all of them came around eventually to the original question: How is the saint to know he is saved? The rhetoric and theology of the Antinomian Controversy were never far away from the immediate problem of providing assurance for the troubled souls of the colonists.

The differences of opinion between the ministers were a serious threat to the unity of Massachusetts so long as Cotton stuck to his position. But at the synod of 1637 he agreed to recognize the validity of the other side; "The Spirit," he now affirmed, "doth Evidence our Justification in both wayes, sometime in an absolute Promise, sometime in a conditionall."

This was really a concession, not a compromise. Though his opponents may have agreed to tolerate Cotton's theology, it was their own synthesis of moralism, activism, and voluntaryism that came to prevail in New England.

In this sense the Antinomian Controversy was a turning point in the religious ideas of the colonists. But the Controversy was not the point at which New England left the mainstream of the Reformed tradition. The Antinomianism of Anne Hutchinson was the real departure, for it prefigured the radical stance of the Quakers. The New England ministers, on the other hand, remained officially faithful to the Westminster Confession for a hundred years. When the liberal movements of the eighteenth century reached New England, they had to do battle with Jonathan Edwards, the greatest champion orthodoxy was to have; and in his *Treatise Concerning Religious Affections*, Edwards quoted more from Thomas Shepard than from any other writer.

The effects of the Antinomian Controversy were rather upon the elusive "temper" of the New England Puritans and the region's church history. In the aftermath of the Controversy, the standards of church membership seemed to need revision, and by the 1640s the ministers were easing the requirement that candidates testify about their experiences. Equally important was the shift in the ministers' thinking about the nature of their authority. The Congregationalism of the thirties was radically experimental in the way it allowed the minister and church members to share authority. But the shock of the Controversy recalled the ministers to a more traditional assertion of their prerogatives. Thus the Congregationalism of the Cambridge Platform (1648) reflected the temper of the forties, just as the Antinomian

Controversy had reflected the temper of the thirties. Gone was the spiritual enthusiasm that had prompted the revival and the experiments in church order. In its place was a formalism that the ministers in New England would lament for another century.

In the preceding essay David Hall related the popularity of Anne Hutchinson's views to the concrete situation of Boston in the mid-1630s. William Stoever is concerned to relate the views of the "Antinomians" to the broader context of Protestant thought of the Reformation. He focuses on John Cotton, the most articulate of those who were identified with the Hutchinsonian faction at the outset of the dispute. Some historians have perceived the orthodox party as attempting innovations in Puritan theology which were protested by Cotton and Anne Hutchinson. Stoever rejects this contention and argues that it was the "Antinomians" who were the radical innovators. Stoever also relates the argument over faith and works to the participants' general perception of the nature of the created world.

WILLIAM K.B. STOEVER

"The Theological Dimension"

• • •

In spite of the rhetoric about "legalism" and "going on in a covenant of works", the Antinomian Controversy at the theological level was not basically about the meriting of grace (in a Roman Catholic sense), or about human cooperation with grace (in an Arminian sense), or about unregenerate ability to "prepare" for "effectual calling" (in the sense of some modern interpreters). Rather, it concerned a broader and more fundamental issue; namely, the proper relationship between created nature and divine activity in the process of regeneration itself. John Winthrop noted that the specific points in dispute were whether the Holy Spirit dwells in believers bodily and whether sanctification may be an evidence of justification. These issues were special cases of the larger one. The elders were guilty neither of making salvation contingent on obedience to the moral law (the terms of the "covenant of works" as enjoined upon Adam), nor of making justification depend upon motions of the unaided human will. They did, however, believe that God in accomplishing regeneration uses "means" which belong to the created order, and respects the inherent capacities of human beings. The dissenters, in contrast, maintained that God acts directly upon men, overruling natural capacities, and transforms men apart from, and in spite of, any activity of theirs. In this disagreement a theological issue of major significance for Puritans, and for Reformed Protestants generally, was at stake.

Much twentieth-century interpretation of the Antinomian Controversy inclines toward the view that the dissenters' judgment of the elders was basically correct. Perry Miller, for example, treated the incident as a dispute over the place of unregenerate human activity, or "natural ability", preparatory to saving conversion, which he regarded as being, properly for Reformed Protestants, exclusively an act of God's sovereignty; "preparation" was the basic, though largely hidden, issue. Edmund Morgan considered Cotton a self-conscious defender of the Protestant principles of human helplessness and divine omnipotence in the face of Arminian-like tendencies among the other elders. Larzer Ziff defined the controversy in terms of "legalism" and a "conditional" understanding of the covenant of grace, in contrast to absolute election and human passivity in regeneration; the issue between Cotton and his colleagues was the "extent to which . . . a man contributed to his salvation." More recently, Norman Pettit developed Miller's notions about preparation into a general interpretation of seventeenth-century theological controversy in New England. In contrast David Hall explained the episode in the context of religious revival and physical privation in the wilderness, identifying the central issue as personal assurance of salvation.

In re-examining the theological dimension of the Antinomian Controversy, one does not wish to dissent entirely from the interpretations just mentioned. At the same time, it may be noted that post-Millerian interpretation, read with attention to the formal divinity of Reformed orthodoxy, which Puritans shared, raises a number of questions about the nature and significance of the New England controversy. These questions fall more or less into three groups.

1. Granting that divine sovereignty and human helplessness in achieving salvation were cardinal points of Reformed doctrine, did this mean that human activity was, as such, excluded entirely from the process of regeneration? And, given that human activity was an issue in the New England controversy, to what extent was it activity specifically in "preparation for conversion"? Events in the Bay Colony in 1636-38 indicate that the answer to the first question was not crystal clear to contemporaries. Analysis of the pertinent theological literature, however, suggests that the opposition between human activity and divine grace was not understood among Reformed divines to be as absolute as Miller and others defined it. Regarding the second question, examination of the principal New England sources suggests, to this writer at least, that "preparation" in 1636-38 was at most an issue only incidentally. Rather, the basic doctrinal issue concerned the place of created human nature vis à vis the increated power of the Trinity in the regenerating transformation itself—a theologically more fundamental and serious matter (though it would have included "preparation" in Miller's sense).

2. The immediate practical context of the controversy between Cotton and

the other ministers, clearly, was the problem of personal assurance of election. In formal Reformed divinity, however, the locus on assurance occupies a definite systematic-theological context in that what is said about evidencing election follows from what is said about the nature of God and how he works in accomplishing regeneration. Accordingly, one may ask, what broader theological resources were available to the ministers for addressing the specific problem of assurance? And how did Cotton's understanding of the systematic context differ from that of his colleagues, such that his approach to assurance appeared radically different?

3. Taking account of the foregoing, how are the principals in the controversy, especially Cotton and the other ministers, to be located in the history of Reformed Protestantism? In particular, to what extent were the New England elders being original in asserting that sanctification might be a necessary and legitimate evidence of justification, and to what degree were they thereby departing from the straight and narrow of the Protestant *sola gratia?*

Each of these questions will be treated in turn. First, however, a word is necessary about the background of the discussion. As theologians, English and New English Puritans belonged to the period of so-called Reformed orthodoxy (roughly 1570-1700), which was primarily concerned with defining Reformed doctrine and articulating it in the intellectual idiom of late scholasticism. While allowing considerable latitude in individual expression, Reformed orthodoxy comprised a rather broad consensus within the Reformed tradition regarding the substance of doctrine and theological method. Orthodoxy's characteristic literary expression was the formal *loci communes*, treating the common "heads" of Reformed divinity systematically arranged. Of examples by Englishmen William Perkins' *Golden Chain* (1591) and William Ames' internationally popular handbook, *Medulla Theologica* (1623), are the best-known. Both were employed in New England, as was Johannes Wollebius' more abbreviated *Compendium Theologiae Christianae* (1626). New England's own contribution to the genre was John Norton's *Orthodox Evangelist* (1654). On the whole, Puritans produced fewer and less substantial systematic works than their continental brethren. Their theological reflection tended instead to take the Form of sermon-cycles on issues of current pastoral or controversial importance which, when published, became part of the theological literature. John Preston's *Breastplate of Faith and Love* (1630), Richard Sibbes' *Soul's Conflict* (1635) and Thomas Shepard's *Sound Believer* (1645) are cases in point. These titles and others, from the pens of what New Englanders called "our standard Reformed divines", form the backdrop for what follows.

I. *Divine sovereignty and human activity.* In the handbooks of divinity the ultimate point of departure for considering regeneration is God regarded in himself; the penultimate point of departure is God considered as he is related to the world. Regarded in himself, God is understood to be one, eternal and immutable, and entirely unconditioned by anything outside of himself. Considered in relation to the world, God is understood as First Cause, as Necessary Being and as Supreme Volition, upon whom all creatures depend for possibility and actuality. As creator, God's power is sufficient to effect

nything which is not logically con-
radictory; yet in creating the actual
vorld, God clearly did not exhaust
he logically possible. This is the
esult, however, solely of his own
ree determination and not of any
nherent impotency or external con-
traint. Reflecting on God's activity
n relation to the world, Reformed
heologians subordinated the divine
ower, as manifest in the actual order
of things, to the divine will, and
listinguished between *potentia dei
absoluta* and *potentia dei ordinata
ive actualis.* The first refers to God's
ower considered in itself, the second
o his power as "limited by his decree
and revealed will: according to which
God having freely bounded himself,
[he] changes not, being immutable."
In speaking of God's "efficiency"
Reformed theologians had in mind
God's power solely in the latter sense.
Accordingly, regeneration is not properly defined in terms of the impinging
of divine omnipotence directly upon
created human nature, but rather in
terms of the operation of omnipotence
toward particular ends and through
appropriate means; and the means as
well as the ends are understood to
be rooted in the same free and un-
alterable divine determination.

In regenerating individuals God
works through the concrete instru-
mentalities of word and sacrament—
the "means of grace" in the narrow
sense. These "means", though they
depend upon God for their effective-
ness, belong to the created order, and
they operate according to their
distinctive natures as created. Divine
grace is conveyed in and through
the words of the sermon, but the
natural operations of speaking and
hearing, and the proper character of
words as vehicles of meaning, are not
altered by their function as vehicles
of grace. In the "golden chain" of

events which issues in the salvation
of particular men, God ordinarily
employs a series of second causes, and
he proceeds in such a way that the
proper agency and characteristic activity of these causes are preserved.
Second causes cannot produce their
effects without the First Cause, but
God will not produce a given effect ·
without the appropriate second causes.
God exercises his efficiency by "moving upon, co-working with, and asisting
of the second cause in its operations."
"God causes the burning of the fire,
yet we do not say God burns, but
the fire burns."

The same is true of the recipient of
grace. "God works repentance in the
soul, yet it is not a truth to say God
repents, but man repents." In attaining his ends God guides creatures by
supplying them with a power and a
manner of working which is suited to
their inherent capacities. Man, alone
of earthly creatures, is able to propose
ends to himself and frame means for
their attainment. In regeneration,
therefore, God moves man by appealing to the understanding with arguments, thereby presenting motives to
the will; and he moves the will according to its nature as a free agent by
supplying it with a gracious power to
will well. The result is that act of
faith by which the soul goes forth to
receive Christ, thereby entering the
covenant of grace and partaking of
its blessings. Faith in the heart,
though its nature is spiritual and its
efficient cause is the Holy Spirit, is
nonetheless a human act. Its "in-
strumental cause" is the word of the
minister, and its form is that of a persuasion, which begins with cognition
and issues in action. The regenerate
sinner is in truth a "new creature", else
he could not believe at all; throughout,
however, he remains fully a human
being, and his spiritual rebirth is

accomplished through the faculties of his distinctively human nature.

> We on the one hand [wrote John Norton] against the Enthusiasts affirm not only the power to use, but the duty of using the means; and on the other hand, against the Arminians deny that man before grace can do anything, having the power of a cause (so far forth as comes from them) in order to life; because we are reasonable creatures God proceeds with us in the use of means; because we are dead creatures, in respect of the efficacy of the means, we depend wholly and absolutely upon God.

In Reformed orthodox divinity the essential gratuity of regeneration derives from its foundation, in all respects, in the free will of God. That God condescends to accommodate the effecting of regeneration to natural human capacities, and to treat with men for salvation in a manner requiring their persuasion and consent, is the result of his own free decision. Justification depends upon the act of faith, but only because God has arbitrarily established such a relationship. Faith does not merit justification; and the act of faith itself springs from a gracious power, added beyond man's natural endowment. At the same time, the integrity of human creatures is upheld in that God "so administers his absolute decree, as that there is as much place left for an efficacious conditional dispensation, as if the decree itself were conditional." And he administers his decree through "means" which belong to the order of second causes acting in accordance with their created natures. In approaching the Antinomian Controversy, it is important to realize the extent to which Reformed divines, including Puritans, sought to hold together divine sovereignty with

human activity, the gratuity of justification with its conditionality, and divine efficiency with the instrumentality of created things—and to do this in a manner which would not sacrifice either the *sola gratia* of the Protestant Reformation, or the Augustinian (and normative Christian) affirmation of the essential goodness of creation.

II. *Assurance and the evidencing of justification.* As Protestants, Puritans insisted that certainty of one's estate may be attained short of heaven. They also maintained that the decree of election is hidden in God's mind, that hypocrites are able to counterfeit all the outward marks of grace, and that subjective awareness of grace varies with a person's moods and the Spirit's motions. A person might diligently attend church, feel deeply penitent and yearn for Christ, and yet not feel certain that he was justified. From the pulpit he was implored to make sure of his estate in grace—and warned, for his soul's safety, against resting in a false or mistaken assurance. Where might a hopeful saint, troubled by doubt and the danger of self-deception, turn for assistance and comfort?

The New England elders replied, let him look to his sanctification. In the gospel "conditional promises" of redemption are made to works of sanctification. If a person finds himself truly humble before God, or longs earnestly to come to Christ, or diligently enjoys all known means of coming, waiting for God to make good his promise of salvation—to each of these "qualifications" a promise is annexed; and if the qualification belongs to a person, the promise does too. Conditional promises are given specifically to aid in identifying the regenerate; their "conditions" are objective signs which indicate the presence of sanctifying grace and by which the redeemed are actually "singled out and marked." In the "application of redemption"—the order God follows in effecting regeneration—sanctification necessarily follows from justification, and so it is possible to conclude from one to the other in a "practical syllogism." In this manner a person may first come to know the blessedness of his estate "by the peculiarness of a work within him."

The elders' cousel to seek comfort in sanctification was not an especially easy one, for it carried a serious qualification touching the "peculiarness" of the "works" in question. Conditional promises are not made to mere outward acts of obedience, which hypocrites can counterfeit, but only to such acts performed from a proper "frame and disposition of the heart." The hopeful saint, therefore, must examine his behaviour rigorously in light of conscience and of God's revealed will. Scripture contains the rule of obedience by which Christians are to walk; and conscience, the faculty of introspection, is privy to human motives, and by it a person may know with what "frame and disposition" of heart he approaches the task of obedience. Right, sincere and sound sanctification, Bulkeley noted, frames the heart to close with the whole will of God in everything a person does. The truly sanctified render universal obedience to God because they delight in thus glorifying him; and they are conscious that their obedience springs from the power of grace, which alone enables them to obey. Though outwardly a man may deceive the keenest observer, inwardly these are the touchstones by which he may know in his heart whether he is only a "close hypocrite."

In urging works of sanctification as evidence of justification, the New England elders maintained, they were not implying that a person might merit justification in a causal sense by doing "good works", but only that such works are "declarative, making manifest who be those true believers to whom the life promised in the covenant doth belong." Justification, which involves no change in the individual but only in God's attitude toward him, is not likely to be *felt* by the justified. But sanctification, the actual infusion of gracious habits, is a positive change in a man's person which manifests itself in distinctive actions and, more importantly, in distinctive motives, which conscience may recognize. Accordingly, a person may take assurance of his justification from the "sight" in himself of works of sanctification to which biblical promises are made or implied. In doing so he is not "closing with Christ", as he does in entering the covenant of grace, but only drawing a reasonable conclusion from empirical evidence interpreted in light of scripture. In this the elders were in accord with the affirmation of Reformed divinity that in regeneration God normally employs created things as means and instruments, and works in a manner appropriate to man's created nature, without therein ceasing to be fully God or fully gracious.

To all of this John Cotton and the Hutchinsonians objected on the ground that works and human activity as such have nothing to do with the accomplishing, or the revealing, of the Spirit's regenerating work, even though such activities be gracious.

In the normative Reformed understanding graces of sanctification inhere in the regenerate, and though they derive their power from the Spirit's sustenance, they are active in the saints themselves. The New England elders were at pains to make clear that the sanctified do not dispose over graces apart from the Spirit's operation, but they were equally insistent that graces of sanctification subsist in, and are active in, regenerate persons, and that the actions which they empower are properly spoken of as the *persons'* actions. Cotton, in contrast, came very close to denying the inherence of graces in the believer. He regarded sanctification as a "positive" change in the regenerate, and he retained the notion of infused graces; but he so emphasized the dependence of graces on Christ's activity as to make their existence in the regenerate merely relative. He flatly denied that graces, of their own power, could "work" in the regenerate.

For Cotton the righteousness of sanctification is not properly men's but Christ's, indeed *is* Christ, who is "made . . . our righteousness and sanctification." All spiritual gifts exist first, and fully, in Christ, whence they are derived by the Spirit's agency to those who are in union with Christ. Graces infused, moreover, "become active and lively not of themselves, but as Christ is active in them and puts forth himself in them day by day." Without Christ's continuous activity in the saints, their gifts would fly away as Adam's did, and leave them naked, though Adam's gifts were perfect. Cotton's colleagues asked him "whether a Christian be not further active after regeneration, than before it?" Cotton replied that a Christian is not at all active before regeneration, but allowed that after it, "acted upon we act." "Come to any holy duty, and it is the Holy Ghost that leads you along, and acts you. . . . It is the Spirit of God that moves us to any good work, and that acts the gifts of his grace in us." Sanctifying graces are not active apart from additional help from Christ to activate them, and there is no possibility of any "active power in us of ourselves through gifts received." With this assertion Cotton

distinguished himself from the tradition of Reformed orthodoxy as received in New England.

The implications of Cotton's position were considerable. If infused graces are unable to empower men's actions, then Christ must somehow enter, or act directly upon, human faculties if individuals are to act holily. To say this, however, was to eliminate any essential difference between the good acts of believers and those of hypocrites, and it was to imply that gracious habits are not really infused into believers—that in effect there is no positive regeneration of *individuals* at all. Furthermore, to suggest that the Spirit acts immediately in sanctification was to admit a degree of commerce between creatures and the Trinity to which the Reformed tradition was uniformly opposed. The elders of the Bay, in accord with that tradition, held that the substance of sanctification is present in believers inherently (though derivatively from Christ), and not accidently and immediately from Christ. They affirmed that the exalted Christ dwells in believers "by his Spirit", but they insisted that Christ's Spirit is present mediately, in and through created graces infused into the soul, which empower the man himself to act. If Christ acts upon believers only by the Spirit's immediate operation, Thomas Shepard wrote,

> then there is seeing in a Christian without an eye, and hearing without an ear, and knowing Christ without an understanding, and loving without love, and living without life, and feeding and eating without a mouth; and then, when these actings are over, a Christian is like another man; there is no law remains written on his heart, and so Christ should enter into his saints, like Satan into the serpent, who only acts the serpent, and when that is done, he remains a serpent again. Know

it, the Lord Jesus his greatest work is not only to change the acts, but to change the heart; not only to put new actions, but a new nature into men.

The alternative was not only contrary to accepted doctrine; it was also hostile to the Puritan endeavor to establish a commonwealth leavened by the presence of truly godly individuals.

Cotton's position on the evidencing of justification was consistent with his assertion of the Spirit's immediate operation in sanctification, and with his devaluation of gracious human activity. He was committed by the received tradition to a positive change in the regenerate, which distinguished them from hypocrites, but he insisted that this change is hidden from creaturely eyes, including the enlightened eyes of a regenerate conscience.

Regeneration, Cotton maintained, is so exalted a transformation that it can be discerned only by an equally exalted means; namely, by the Spirit's own testimony "without respect to a work", that is, "without sight of any work of ours." When pressed, he allowed that an enlightened conscience could discern whether a man's sanctification were true, but only if the observation of conscience were based on the Spirit's testimony and only if the conclusion followed from "spiritual sight" of one's interest in Christ—which was, in effect, to deny the point. Prior to the Spirit's witness, Cotton maintained, a person may have "knowledge" of his justification by means of the "created spiritual light abiding in the regenerate conscience", such knowledge being a deduction from observable data in light of the rule of scripture. This, however, is really no knowledge at all, since it falls infinitely short of that "faith of assurance" of justification which can only come from "an immediate light of the Spirit

of God above the letter of the word, and above the created light of conscience." Neither sincere faith in Christ, as a human act, nor free and hearty obedience to divine commands, is able to provide the soul with settled comfort "until the Spirit of Christ doth witness to the soul God's peace toward himself", and this "by immediate light from himself." "Immediately I say, though not without the word of God nor without (sometimes in some cases) the work of God, yet with his own immediate power above the power which either the word hath of itself, or the work of any creature." To see by an enlightened conscience a work in oneself, and a promise made to it in scripture, and to take confidence from thence that one is justified—such can only be to "go on in a covenant of works", for "such faith is not the work of God's power begotten by the divine testimony and operation of the Spirit of God (for it is before it), but hammered it is and engendred out of the concourse of three creatures."

Cotton's colleagues also regarded the "clearing of our spiritual estate" to be the Spirit's work. The issue was by what means of objective word and sensible work the Spirit in fact bears witness. The elders held that he accomplishes it through that "created spiritual light" which enables the regenerate to perceive the excellency of Christ, the truth of their own justification and the soundness of their sanctification. For Cotton the operation of God's almighty power and the capacities of created things were incompatible, and the latter could not be the vehicle of the former, even in a practical syllogism.

Was assurance the work of a gracious human spirit, and so a human work, or a work of the Spirit himself, and so a divine one? That was the question. Before the Boston church Anne

Hutchinson was charged with maintaining that "the first thing we receive for our assurance is our election" (as a direct testimony of the Spirit). The ministerial synod, meeting at Cambridge in August and September 1637, condemned the notions that "no created work can be a manifest sign of God's love" (taken as referring to such created graces as love to the brethren), and that "nothing but Christ is an evidence of my good estate" (understood in reference to the opposition between Christ "manifesting himself in works of holiness" and "Christ nakedly revealing himself to faith"). Cotton held that conscious faith follows justification in the application of regeneration, and understood "justifying faith" to be the assurance by which a believer knows himself to be justified. Commenting on the latter notion, Bulkeley identified the fundamental issue in the New England controversy:

> This is some of that new light which the old age of the Church hath brought forth; which what it tends unto, I know not, unless it be to this, that a man should not look at any habitual grace in himself, whether sanctification or faith, or any other, in as much as these avail nothing (according to them) to a man's justification, seeing we are justified before faith: They would have a man to see nothing in himself, because (as they think) *the grace which is seen is temporal, that grace which is not seen is eternal.*

In other words, grace which is subject to empirical observation, as something belonging to the created order, is qualitatively different from grace which is dispensed immediately by the Holy Spirit in his own person. Anne Hutchinson allegedly held that "there are no created graces in . . . believers after union [with Christ]." Cotton

maintained that the agency, instrumentality and activity of creatures, including gracious habits, are incidental to the Spirit's work in regeneration. For Cotton, as for Mistress Anne, the basic opposition lay not between "nature" and the "supernatural" (in the modern sense), nor between "corrupt nature" (of fallen man) and "saving grace," but—what was more radical and theologically more serious—between created being as such and the increated being of the Trinity.

The key to the issue lies in the Hutchinsonian reference, above, to "created graces", in Cotton's opposition between "created" and "immediate" light, and in Bulkeley's contrast between "temporal" and "eternal" grace. The distinction between created and increated nature was employed in Reformed divinity to discriminate between the being and activity of God, which are necessary, and the contingent being and activity of everything else: for example, heaven, earth, animate and inanimate beings, the biblical word, the preaching of law and gospel and the habits of faith and sanctification. Such habits, which God gratuitously infuses into the soul, are distinctive in that they are contrary to fallen human nature, and are beyond the attainment of natural human capacities. But inasmuch as gracious habits are contingent in both existence and activity—being gifts of God and not God himself—they belong to the created order. The grace bestowed in regeneration is thus "created" and "temporal." Reformed orthodox divines insisted that men are saved "by grace alone", but they also maintained that God in bestowing grace works mediately, through created instruments, including infused habits. Cotton and the Hutchinsonians, in contrast, held that "by grace alone" excludes created means, and that the

Spirit, accordingly, must act upon (or simply "act") men directly. They tended therefore severely to minimize, if not actually to deny, the instrumentality of created things; and they asserted that in accomplishing and revealing regeneration, the Spirit operates directly upon the individual's mind and will. From the perspective of the received theological tradition this was an illegitimate subordination of created nature to the increated power of the Trinity.

III. *Historical assessment.* . . . It is at least possible that, in dealing with Cotton and the Hutchinsonians, the New England elders were asserting what they conscientiously regarded as proper Reformed doctrine, in the face of what they correctly perceived to be sectarian tendencies. In England by the 1630s the phrase "free justification by grace alone" (and variants) was acquiring the character of a party slogan. Often it appears less as a conscientious appeal to the cardinal principles of the Reformation than as the rallying cry of assorted nonconformists whose common characteristic was unusual intimacy with the Holy Spirit, to the ultimate subordination of all creaturely activity. In New England in 1636-38 the phrase served (though not in all instances) as the positive polemical counterpart to the charge of "preaching", "being under", or "going aside to" a covenant of works. Protestations about devotion to "free grace", however, may serve to conceal incipient sectarianism as well as to evidence doctrinal purity; and this ambiguity, together with the usage of the phrase in contemporary English sectarianism, suggests that claims for the normative Protestantism of the New England dissenters should be accepted with reservation. In any case, neither Luther nor Calvin in-

tended the *sola gratia* to mean that God, in acting graciously, violates the ontological order established at creation; and both Reformers actively opposed those who, in the name of "free grace", would dissolve the infinite qualitative difference between creatures and the Persons of the Trinity.

Examined in the context of contemporary Reformed divinity, the theological evidence suggests less that the elders of the Bay Colony were crypto-Arminians, undermining the *sola gratia* by slight concessions to unregenerate human agency, than that Cotton in 1636 was a crypto-sectary, perilously close to invalidating creaturely agency altogether, of both biblical word and regenerate work, in the name of the unconditioned, increated agency of the Trinity. Moreover, on their own ground at least, the New England elders were right to take alarm, for the issues raised in the Antinomian Controversy went to the center of the Puritan enterprise. In his insistence on the priority of the Spriit's immediate operation, Cotton upset the careful dialectic of nature and grace which informed Puritanism's effort to gather churches of the truly regenerate, as against the merely baptized, and which also informed the Puritan endeavor to establish earthly societies at once truly godly and fully participant in political, social and economic life. Without entering upon the question of causal priority, it remains that Puritanism's concrete efforts radically to transform men and institutions, and yet not dissolve the social order, were both legitimated and moderated by the theological conviction that God in attaining his ends employs means which belong to the created order and employs them according to their natural capacities.

All of the Puritan immigrants to the New England colonies believed that the course of history was laid out according to a divine plan. History began with Adam and moved providentially towards the triumphant second coming of Christ and the millenial rule of the saints. The spiritual progress of the individual duplicated that of the world. But there was room for debate over the details involved in this general pattern. Did the redeemed world become a new Eden or assume an entirely unprecedented character? Did the redeemed soul become a new Adam, or did it assume the image of Christ? Jesper Rosenmeier approaches the Antinomian controversy from this perspective and highlights a different religious theme than that of Stoever's essay. Yet Rosenmeier is dealing with some ideas that do suggest comparison with Stoever's article. Are the two selections complementary?

JESPER ROSENMEIER

''The Image of Adam and the Image of Christ''

The Puritans who sailed from Plymouth, England, in April 1630 were confident that with them into the wilderness went God'd promises of the world. In his farewell sermon, "Gods Promise to His Plantation," John Cotton had assured them that whatever hazards and tribulations were in store for them, they could rest confident that the society they would plant after their exodus would serve as a great example to a continent engaged in the bloody Thirty Years Wars, and to an England where Antichrist daily seemed to gain power. In the first years, the New England Puritans' expectations for their plantations seemed to be justified. Cotton, who came across to Massachusetts in the early fall of 1633, wrote to his good friend, John Davenport, then in Holland but soon to come to Boston, that "the Order of the Churches and of the Commonwealth was so settled, by common Consent, that it brought to his mind, the New Heaven and New Earth, wherein dwells Righteousness."

The initial harmony did not last long. By 1634 differences had appeared that within two years would divide Massachusetts into two major factions. On one side of the house divided stood Cotton, the teacher of the First Church; Sir Henry Vane, the new governor; John Wheelwright, minister at Mount Wollaston; and most of the Boston congregation, among them Anne Hutchinson and her family. Cotton's and Vane's party also had scattered support in Salem, Newbury, Roxbury, Ipswich, and Charlestown. On the other side were Cotton's colleague, John Wilson, pastor of the First Church; John Winthrop, the former governor; and a few others from the Boston congregation. Yet—and this was to be conclusive for the outcome of the controversy—Wilson and Winthrop could count on the support of all the other elders and most of the people in the towns surrounding Boston. Especially valuable among the elders was Thomas Shepard, the young minister of the church in Cambridge, and, next to Cotton, the finest theologian and most effective preacher in the Bay.

• • •

In the context of our increased interest in the theological issues of the Crisis, the recent publication of a debate between Cotton, the teacher to the First Church in Boston, and the other elders in the Bay is of the highest significance, for the debate elucidates our understanding of the Crisis in two major respects. First, the argument when unfolded helps us identify *the* central issue, and, second, helps us place the whole Antinomian Crisis—more properly it should be called the Familist Crisis—in its context. With the help of the debate we come to see vividly the elements of the division in that pure Christian church set up in Massachusetts to serve as the great example to all the world.

. . . In the final section of the debate, "Mr. Cottons Revisall," Cotton provides a summary of his beliefs. As the debate moves through this five-layered dialogue the arguments are wonderfully clarified and refined. In the process, the issue that emerges as everybody's central concern is seen in question nine in which the other elders ask Cotton, almost accusingly, what he takes to be the meaning of *"Christian Sanctification"*; whether, as they have heard rumored but can scarcely believe, he means by sanctification *"the immediate acting"* of the Holy Spirit or, as they would prefer to think, *"infused* Habits." Their question becomes a hasty reassertion of their own views, ending with the force of a plea: surely *"you must . . . meane the Image of God in* Adam *renewed in us, to be our Sanctification?"* In his answer Cotton chooses to meet the issue head on. "I meane by Christian Sanctification," he says, "the fruit of the Spirit of Christ dwelling in true Beleevers working and acting in us." As part of the work of the Holy Spirit, he includes "both infused *Habits* and actions of *Holinesse,* contrary to all vitious *Habits* and actions of corrupt *Nature.*" "And yet," he states categorically, "the Image of God in *Adam* renewed in us" is not adequate to accomplish Christian sanctification. "Our Sanctification in Christ," he writes, "hath in it this more; Faith in the Righteousnesse of Christ, and Repentance from dead Works, (and that which is the Root of both) the indwelling Power of the Spirit, to act and keep Holinesse in us all, which Adam wanted." For all participants in the debate, it is clear that the questions of the relationship of faith to works and of the role of the Holy Spirit are subordinate to the question of the nature of man's present and future renewal in God's image. Indeed, not only in the debate but throughout the entire Crisis the question of Christian sanctification is primary and it embraces not just the individual's salvation but the redemption of the world as well. At stake in the debate about the image of Adam and the image of Christ is no less than the nature of Christ's kingdom on earth and of the future eternal life, for what is enacted in the microcosm of each man's soul is a perfect reflection of God's work in the macrocosm. All the New England Puritans agreed that the perfection of the world was the *"inheritance"* which awaited them in the wilderness but each side saw differently how the perfection would come about. Further, when we realize that the Puritans expected God's work of redemption to be consummated within a few years, we begin to comprehend the intensity with which they argued. Believing the fate of the world to depend on their answers to the question of man's and the world's rebirth all sides held tenaciously to their separate views, and, up to a point, reached desperately for reconciliation.

To reestablish the spiritual harmony of their first four years in Massachusetts, it was necessary in the debate first to define the differences which separated them. The elders had made the exodus from England convinced that a return to Adam's innocence in the Garden of Eden would be the final state of Christian redemption for the individual as well as for the world. The paradise Adam had lost, they would regain. When Cotton arrived in Boston in 1633, they had greeted him with open arms, but since then they had become increasingly aware that in his teachings "darkly and doubtfully delivered," Cotton was holding forth a very different course and end to their errand. His first answer to their ninth question had not satisfied them, and they asked him if he would explain

more clearly his idea of Christian sanctification. In his answer in *Mr. Cottons Rejoynder*, Cotton insisted that in the engraving of Christ's image on the soul, an entirely new creation takes place. Christian sanctification, he repeated, did not signify a mere restoration to old Adam's innocence but a new and richer holiness embracing faith, repentance, and the indwelling power of the Holy Spirit. The new image was of the crucified and resurrected Christ, not Adam in "the roial seat of *Eden*."

• • •

To the elders, Cotton's teachings opened a frightening perspective of the future. The great point of the history of redemption, they asserted, was that Christ in His sacrifice had paid the penalty for the fall thereby enabling man to return to Adam's original holiness. Rather than as a safe return to a lost but recoverable past, Cotton envisaged history as a never ceasing creation moving towards its culmination in the New Jerusalem with no other guide than the image of Christ's Crucifixion and Resurrection. For the elders this view was both dangerous and insufficient. If Adam's original obedience to God in the covenant of works did not still hold as the cardinal test of Christian holiness, what other ways would there be for good Christians to find assurance of their salvation? To make the test of holiness depend initially on an experiential knowledge of the work of the Holy Spirit, as Cotton did when he said, "I take the *seal* of the *Spirit* to be nothing else but the *Spirit* itself," was to invite uncertainty, indefiniteness, and chaos. A host of self-chosen saints would proclaim that they had experienced Christ's new creation when it was perfectly obvious to men of sober and reasonable judgment that they had not. As evidence that anarchy would be the result of Cotton's preaching, the elders pointed to the views Anne Hutchinson and her followers were spreading. While claiming that they taught nothing their beloved teacher had not first held forth as proper doctrine, their arrogance and defiance of God's appointed magistrates and ministers daily increased. The elders insinuated that Cotton had gone so far toward familism that he could no longer distinguish sound doctrine from false. To persuade Cotton to be "the happy Instrument of calming these storms and cooling these hot contentions and paroxysms that have begun to swell and burn in these poor Churches." the elders used all "private brotherly meanes." But to no avail; Cotton remained adamant. Finding "no healing" with him, they then began to preach openly "both against opinions publikly and privately maintayned." The chief spokesman for Winthrop and the elders became the young minister in Cambridge, Thomas Shepard. In two major series of sermons, the *Theses Sabbaticae,* preached at Harvard College to the future ministers of New England, and *The Parable of the Ten Virgins Opened and Applied,* delivered to the Cambridge Church, Shepard set forth those views concerning the individual and collective renewal of man in Adam's image which would finally prove victorious in the controversy, and which New England would adopt as official doctrine.

In England, Shepard had preached that Adam when he "came first out of Gods mint, shined most glorious." In his "perfection of Holinesse," he mirrored God Himself. "Privie to Gods excellency," Adam loved God as fiercely "as Iron put into the fire seemes to be nothing but fire," and being "a lumpe of love," Adam's body "was a Lanthorne through which Holinesse like a lampe burning in his heart

shined." "Methinks," Shepard exclaimed, "I see Adam wrapt up in continuall extasies in having this God." God's image was Adam's "Stocke and Patrimony" to convey to his posterity and had he not fallen, man would have known "no sorrow, no sicknesse, no teares, no feares, no death, no hell." But when Adam went "Banquerupt" he and all his future children on earth became subject to God's wrath.

Yet in spite of His wrath, God decided to save man, "to get this Image . . . renewed againe," and as the first major step towards the restoration of man's lost holiness, God gave the ten commandments to Moses. The decalogue, Shepard preached at Harvard in the 1630s, "is nothing else but the Law of nature revived, or a second edition and impression of that primitive and perfect law of nature, which in the state of innocency was engraven upon mans heart, but now againe written upon Tables of stone, by the finger of God. For man being made in the Image of God, he had therefore the law of holines and righteousnes, in which Gods Image consisted, written in his heart." Although Shepard shares the general belief that the old dispensation had come to an end with the birth of Christ, and that Christians had succeeded Jews as the chosen people, he maintains, nevertheless, that the great end of the history of redemption remains the return to Adam's original estate. As he told New England's future ministers, "although our original perfection is now defaced and lost . . . yet it had once a being, and therefore in his controversie we may lawfully enquire after it." Consequently, he believes, when the saints are reborn they recover Adam's obedience to the natural law as well as his power of holy action. This renewal is not complete in a man's earthly life, but it is sufficient to carry him "toward his end." The difference between Adam in Paradise and Shepard's renewed Christian in New England is one of degree only:

•••

Usually, Shepard's believer is not aware of the moment when the Holy Spirit acts. Unlike Cotton, as we shall see, Shepard insists that the actual creation of faith in the heart need not be experienced. It suffices to know that love now resides and acts within, that the gracious work has been done. It is not necessary to be feelingly present when God infuses the habits of grace. Look at the good fruits, Shepard exhorts, and if you find them, trust that God created them. . . . Except in rare cases, Christians know their new inward creation not in moments of *"Balaamitish* ravishments, and hypocritical pangs, and land-flood affections" but by reasonably deducing that behind the good works lies grace abiding.

It is this idea of the source of the new creation which radically separates Shepard's and Cotton's preachings on the image of God. Shepard's view makes it unnecessary for him to hold up the image of Christ's Crucifixion and Resurrection as the mirror of the future. The image of the Crucifixion may well be a way station in the voyage back to our "primitive and perfect estate," but it forms no part of the final image. Beyond the Cross and the Ascension, Eden beckons. "What hath God done," he exclaims," but opened the way to the Tree of life, and let you into Paradise again?" Although Shepard could say, "I know there is a difference between *Adams* power to act, which had no Faith, and ours, that hath," and although he could speak as movingly as Cotton about the image of Christ, yet it is Christ as the means to Adam's holiness which he exhorts his congregation to seek:

•••

For all his protestations against "the great plot of Arminians to make Christ a means onely, to make every man a first *Adam*," Shepard comes close to expressing such a view. Of course, he is no outright Arminian. He vehemently denies man's ability to initiate his own salvation, and, like the elders, he insists that *human* works—as distinct from the Spirit's works—must never be taken as first evidence of the presence of grace. Yet, even so, Shepard's faith is that however faint God's impression in the wax of the heart may be, if it can be detected, and detected by the human eye, it evidences the presence of the Spirit:

•••

Shepard does not start his convert on the road to salvation by first exhibiting to him a source of grace outside of men. He circumscribes his offer of Christian liberty by first asking for the fulfilment of what amounts to a commandment: "Look, perceive, discover, view, labor, obey." In the beginning of God's first creation was the Word; in the beginning of Shepard's new creation is the work.

•••

Like his contemporaries, Shepard viewed the individual's salvation as a representation on a small scale of the redemption of the world. Whatever happened in each man's soul had its clear analogies in God's universal drama which since 4004 B.C. had been unfolding until, as foretold in the prophetic books of the Old and New Testaments, it now approached Christ's Second Coming. Christ's return, Shepard believes, will not usher in a millennium; the history of redemption will proceed directly to the day of judgment, when Christ will separate the sheep from the goats: . . . Shepard's sincere convert lives in daily expectation of the end of the world. Shepard does not believe in the possibility of a kingdom preceding the end. . . .

Such a view of the history of redemption makes God's work in the first week of creation the pattern for all stages in history. All later revelations of God's grace and love for man, including Christ's incarnation, are seen as reenactments of the first great creation. The world will never know more love than it did once. On the first sabbath, God laid the copestone on creation; the universe was done and finished. Before the fall, Adam had perfect and perpetual holiness, and when the saint is restored he is filled, even if but in part, with the same holiness. Christ does not break into the established order of salvation and offer a new reality. The new man but resurrects the old; Christ does not stand opposite to Adam. Shepard does not envision history as progressing toward the birth of new and unknown worlds; he thinks of time in all its manifestations as flowing like a river in a circle back to God's first eternity.

• • •

The return to paradise! For the first settlers, the wilderness itself held little interest; their efforts were devoted to gathering the pure church who would hear the cry of Christ's midnight coming. And even as their energies turned to the land itself, Shepard's view of creation, shared by the majority of the people in New England's first generation, would serve as one of two major modes of ordering experience in seventeenth-century America. The saint who had been renewed in Adam's image had recovered his original perception of nature. Once more, the Spirit had created within him the ability to see the harmony between the image of God in his heart and the image of God in nature. Just as the source of nature's life—the first cre-

ation—"is an inward principle of motion in its own place; as the sun and trees, and grass, and cattle," so the "actions" of the second creation "issue" from "the inward principle of Spirit and graces." Rightly perceived, nature emblemized a Christian's faith. Trees and rivers, meadows and mountains spoke of righteousness and grace, meekness, and majesty. As he labored in God's New English vineyard, the Puritan Adam could find in his sowing and reaping emblems of God's first creation and of the planting of New England which would be perfected in the harvest of His jubilee.

While Shepard was preaching to the Cambridge congregation that their paradise would be regained in America, Cotton was promising his Boston saints a very different end to their errand into the wilderness. Not Adam's Eden, an old world, but Christ's kingdom, a new world, would crown the history of redemption. In his farewell sermon, he had mapped out the land of special promise awaiting the saints beyond the Atlantic Ocean, and now, three years after his own settling in Boston, he explained how and when this new world would come into being. He did not oppose the elders' view that the history of redemption would be fulfilled when men returned to their state as images and likenesses of God, and he also fervently hoped Christ would choose the New England churches as his virgin brides at the great marriage of the Lamb which heralded a New Heaven and a New Earth. It was for that purpose God had brought them to New England. Yet Cotton believed that when God closed the circle of redemption and brought man home unto Himself, man would stand before Him as a different creation than he did in the beginning. "Minted" in Adam's innocence, he would come back "engraven" with Christ's image of death and ressurrection.

For Cotton, the elders' view of man's renewal repudiated Christ's image as the mirror of the present and future life. Why, if God thought men could be saved by renewal in Adam's image, had He not sent another Adam, exactly like the first one, whose perfect holiness men could imitate, and who would provide them with the power necessary for holy action? The obvious reason God had sent Christ and not Adam was that He found the old image inadequate. The old creation, Cotton insisted, had been shattered beyond the possibility of restoration. To maintain, as the elders did, that Christ's sacrifice provided the means to return to Adam's primitive estate was, Cotton thought, to say that the innocence which had been lost once and for all could be recaptured. But how could what had once been broken be found whole again, exactly as it was? . . .

For Cotton, Christian rebirth is in two ways a new creation. New and unlike any other creation is the soul's apprehension of the moment when the Holy Spirit engraves Christ's image on his heart and makes the believer a "new hearted" Christian; and equally new are the qualities which the Spirit creates within him. In addition to faith, repentance, and the indwelling power of the Holy Spirit, the new qualities include, Cotton told the elders, "our conformity and likeness to him in his death and resurrection. . . . And our likeness to him in his death and resurrection consisteth in our dying to sin and to this world and to the Law and to ourselves."

What made any real compromise between Cotton and the elders impossible was his view of the role of the Holy Spirit in renewal. When the elders told him that the Holy Spirit acted as "the procreant and conservant cause and not the material of our Sanctification," they meant, as Shepard so painstakingly had worked out, that the Holy Spirit creates and conserves the qualities which distinguish a Christian. When a man was sanctified, it was sufficient for him, they thought, to see only the fruits of the Holy Spirit's activity; it was not necessary to feel the Spirit as a continuous presence in the soul. Cotton, on the other hand, believed that a man's experience of his rebirth is first a consciousness of the Spirit breathing new life into his heart. When the moment is deeply felt and lived, no man doubts that he has been brought to life and is no longer walking "in the congregation of the dead." Just as a man knows his birth in the moment of being born so he knows his rebirth in the moment of resurrection from spiritual death. In both births, a believer acknowledges an agency greater than and outside of man. He was not self-created; he will not be self-saved.

• • •

Although Cotton finds the fallen and the new creations as different as death and life, he does regard them as similar in one important respect: both are created by the Spirit without preceding works. As the first creation, being "without form and void" was given life when God's Spirit moved over the waters and said "let there be light," so the new man and new world are born out of the void of death when Christ the Word is breathed into the soul. . . . In the first creation, after the Holy Spirit had made Adam's nature in God's perfect image, His presence was no longer required. Possessing a natural holiness, Adam needed no outside assistance to fulfil God's commandments, and the Holy Spirit withdrew from His finished work. Not being ingrained in Adam's constitution, the Holy Spriit was unable to prevent the destruction of Adam's holiness. "As soon as ever he had tasted of the forbidden fruit," Adam was left "naked and desperate," for though his *"gifts* were in perfection, yet not having the *Holy Ghost* to *keep* them for him, they all flie from him." Because the Holy Spirit dwells continuously in the Christian believer, his sanctification, Cotton says, becomes a far more divine work than Adam's simple holiness. In the creation of Christ's image, the Spirit does not act once and then leave; He stays and upholds His work of redemption. The new man is God's continuous creation, at all times dependent on the power dwelling within him.

• • •

In the new order of creation, the free sight of grace is the first a man knows of his redemption; his rebirth begins with the gift of liberty, not with the threat of death:

• • •

When the Spirit stamps Christ on the soul, a man does not first see his ability to believe; he first feels an entirely new person inhabiting his flesh. With St. Paul, he exclaims, "Not I but Christ liveth in me." Before man loves God, God loves man. It is not man who accepts Christ, but the living Christ within who accepts man and gives him liberty. "Men," Cotton said, "are not brought to mourn after Christ or for him till after a gracious sight of him, wrought by the Spirit of Grace." Here, in the debate, the bitterness between Cotton and the elders surfaces as he dismisses their teachings as clothing "unwholsome and Popish doctrin with Protestant and wholsome words."

If a man is reborn when he sees the new man, Christ, living within, then all the later promises of salvation given to a Christian are made to the new Christ engraven in the heart, and not, as Shepard believes, to the man himself. "All the promises," Cotton writes, "are given to Christ, and all the conditions are fulfilled in Christ, and the revealing of both is by the revealing of Christ, given of grace freely to the Soul . . . I do believe, . . . Christ is the first and last condition of the promises." As Christ is the first and last condition for the individual believer, so He is the beginning and end of the history of redemption. When all the promises have been fulfilled in Him, God's history will be at an end.

When Cotton speaks of the blessedness awaiting the saints in the imminent millennium, he does not mean a state of future bliss in which the experience and knowledge of suffering has been obliterated. The image of fulfilment that the Holy Spirit engraves in the heart is of the crucified *and* resurrected Christ.

• • •

When the Word lights on the believer and wounds him, the Spirit brings him a realization that it is his sins which have nailed and continue to nail Christ to the cross. . . . The Spirit's wounding of the heart is deadly *and* kind, for the death is followed by an equally powerful experience of rebirth. This double state of mortification and vivification—of crucifixion and resurrection—never ceases. A believer does not feel the Spirit's wounding him only once in his life after which he leaves sorrow behind, looking back to his first sight of Christ's Crucifixion as a never-to-be-repeated act. Having been reborn in Christ's double image, a Christian continues to mirror His Passion. In every moment of his life, death and rebirth are inseparably joined in his heart.

• • •

Cotton's decline from eminence was precipitated by Mrs. Hutchinson's arrival in Boston in 1634. From her own testimony we know that while in England she had been inspired by Cotton's preaching, that she had despaired when he left for Massachusetts, and that, in her desolation the Holy Spirit had given her comfort in a direct illumination which had endowed her, she thought, with the ability to discern who were the prophets of light and who the prophets of darkness.

• • •

This direct revelation had impelled her to follow Cotton to New England, for he above all others, she thought, spoke the "clear ministry" which exhibited Christ come in the flesh. Yet in a short time, she had gone far beyond Cotton's teachings. In Boston's isolated and intensely millennial atmosphere, she began to proclaim that the kingdom of Christ had indeed already come. Not satisfied with waiting for Christ's coming she craved nothing less than an immediate and complete union with Christ. At her Church trial in 1638, when the issues of the 1636 debate were still festering, John Wilson asked her, "What doe we mene by the Cominge of Christ Jesus?" And she answered, "By the Cominge of Christ . . . he meanes his *cominge to us in Union.*" Her answer angered and frightened the ministers. Traditionally Christ's Second Coming had been interpreted as the last event in the history of redemption. As we have seen, many Christians believed, as did Cotton, that as the first step in the Second Coming, Christ would set up a kingdom on earth which would last for a millennium, after which he would reappear at the resurrection of the body and the day of judgment. Others believed as Shepard did that the millennium was already past. But all agreed that the Second Coming lay in the future.

Therefore, when Mrs. Hutchinson proclaimed Christ's coming accomplished in His union with her, she was not only telling the ministers that New England's errand had been run but the history of redemption had ended, and the day of jubilee was at hand. Had the ministers allowed her to have her way, their own model of Christ's kingdom would have had to be discarded. "If thear be no Resurection," Cotton told her in his final but by then futile admonition, "than all is vayne, and we of all people are most miserable."

• • •

As fantastic as her revelations were, the civil and ecclesiastical authorities were afraid that unless she were stopped from speaking what they considered heresies, the present social order would give way to a society where no authority would be recognized at all. Winthrop had built his Christian city on the assumption that it would be a beacon guiding the rest of the world; he did not think that the new Jerusalem had yet descended on Boston. If complete union with Christ were possible in this world, what need then to obey magistrates? What need to follow the law if the Holy Spirit had made you so perfect that you could do no wrong? The result would be the "most desperate enthusiasm in the world." No woman would obey her husband, no child his parent, no servant his master. Ministers would be superfluous. The family of love, that very perversion of Christ's kingdom, would spring up where now the covenanted society ruled: "The filthie Sinne of the Comunitie of Woemen and all promiscuus and filthie cominge togeather of men and Woemen without Distinction or Relation of Marriage, will necessarily follow. . . . The Lawfullness of the common use of all Weomen and soe more dayngerous

Evells and filthie Unclenes and other sines will follow than you doe now Imagine or conceave."

Faced with the threat from Anne Hutchinson and her followers, the magistrates acted quickly to protect Christ's new plantations from becoming families of free love. In November 1637 she was banished from the Bay. She was allowed to stay until the following spring because she was expecting a child, but in March 1638, after her excommunication from the Boston Church, she left for Providence. The immediate crisis had passed and the victory was Winthrop's and Shepard's. The New England saints were directed to fix their sights on the day of doom and the eternal paradise. Cotton's way to the New Jerusalem had been discredited. His belief in the power of the Holy Spirit to make men and women prophets of new wine by direct revelation made him defend Mrs. Hutchinson long after it had become clear to everybody else that she was Satan's instrument for the destruction of New England.

For the moment Cotton stood eclipsed. Yet his teachings had been planted too firmly to be uprooted. In succeeding generations there would be many who, rejecting Shepard's as well as the familists' views, would turn to that image of life Cotton preached in the 1630s.

The Trial

Edmund S. Morgan is one of the most respected historians of early America, whose works on Puritan New England include *Visible Saints*, *Roger Williams: The Church and the State*, and *The Puritan Family*. In this article he explains the nature of Puritan views on the character of political society and governmental authority. He demonstrates how Anne Hutchinson posed a threat to these concepts and how, from the Puritan viewpoint, it was necessary to proceed against her. The success of their entire venture in the wilderness required firm action.

EDMUND S. MORGAN

"The Case Against Anne Hutchinson"*

The tercentenary year of the founding of the Massachusetts Bay Colony saw the publication of three biographies of Anne Hutchinson, all of which eulogized the lady at the expense of the colony's orthodox governors. Winnifred Rugg proclaimed her the "mother of the twentieth-century woman," "a lonely exemplar in newborn America of that freedom of thought, word, and action that women now accept as unthinkingly as the air they breathe." Edith Curtis averred that for a long period "almost the sole contribution that Massachusetts made to American civilization" was in the struggle for civil liberty against Governor Winthrop and his successors, begun by Mrs. Hutchinson. Helen Augur declared that although Winthrop was moved by sincere convictions, "he could not recognize in Anne Hutchinson's teachings the outlines of another religious and political philosophy with its own right to exist."

Miss Augur implies, of course, that we should recognize this at once. Indeed, all these biographies are flattering to the modern reader; for they are based on an assumption, which we also

*Abridged, with permission, from original article appearing in the New England Quarterly.

accept as unthinkingly as the air we breathe, that we are not only modern but also enlightened. Each of them seems to say that we have made such "progress" since the age of the Puritans that we can understand both the Puritans and persons like Anne Hutchinson who were "in advance" of that age. We have gone forward so far that we can even accord a certain condescending sympathy to the orthodox Puritans themselves. That they were inferior, however, in breadth of perception to the prophet of liberalism, Anne Hutchinson, we should never doubt for a moment. This is the implication of these three biographies published on the three-hundredth anniversary of the founding of Massachusetts.

The three-hundredth anniversary of the banishment of Mrs. Hutchinson is an opportune moment to say a few words in explanation of her treatment by Massachusetts. Without attempting to palliate the unfairness of her trial, it may be of some value to recall the mental climate in which it was conducted. For such a change has come over our ways of thinking since the seventeenth century that it is difficult for us to understand the issues involved in her condemnation.

• • •

Although the Puritans showed some awareness of, and respect for, the sort of truth attainable by observation of the world, they were still chiefly medieval in their theory of knowledge. They believed that absolute truth, of which, they said, nature gives only a hint, was revealed to man once and for all in the Word of God, the Bible. At the Reformation, Calvin had rejected the interpretation of the Bible used by the Catholic Church and had made a complete interpretation of his own. Since that time, two generations of Puritans had been revising Calvin's

interpretation, and this revision for them was absolute truth, divine and unquestionable. It was not merely the statement of things as they are in the world; it was truth eternal, unlimited by time or space. It was the way of salvation. By it the Puritans had determined to mold their daily lives, their church, and their state. And to make this determination a reality they had crossed the Atlantic and had settled on the shores of Massachusetts Bay.

While they were still maintaining a precarious existence, Anne Hutchinson joined them. At first she was welcomed as the godly wife of a pious and successful merchant; but before she had been long in Massachusetts, she broached a doctrine which was absolutely inconsistent with the principles upon which the colony had been founded. She began to affirm a new basis for absolute truth: immediate personal communion with the Holy Ghost. If this communion had been merely for the purposes of illuminating the meaning of Holy Scripture, the Puritans might have had no quarrel with her. The communion which she described, however, was one which resulted in immediate revelation apart from the Word. To accept her doctrine would mean the abandonment of the fundamental belief for which the Puritans had crossed the water—the belief that truth for man was to be found in the Bible. It would mean a complete change in their daily lives, in their church, and in their state.

As for their daily life, the Puritans saw that the new doctrine would probably encourage or condone indolence and loose-living. In the communion described by Mrs. Hutchinson the believer was completely passive. He did not scrutinize his life to see whether it was in accord with the precepts of the Bible; he merely waited for the Holy Ghost. As Thomas Welde put it, "he is to stand still and waite for Christ to doe all for him. . . . And if he fals into sinne, he is never the more disliked of God, nor his condition never the worse." This would remove all the rational basis for moral endeavor which the Puritan theologians had been painfully constructing since the time of Calvin. The magistrates of Massachusetts found an example of what acceptance of this heresy meant in the refusal of Mrs. Hutchinson's followers to join the expedition against the Pequots.

As for the church, the Puritans must have realized that Mrs. Hutchinson's dogma destroyed most of the reasons for its existence. For in the list of eighty-two errors refuted by a synod of New England ministers, and declared by most members of the court which condemned her to have sprung from her doctrine of revelation, are found these two statements:

> Errour 22. None are to be exhorted to beleeve, but such whom we know to be the elect of God, or to have his Spirit in them effectually.
> Error 53. No Minister can teach one that is annoynted by the Spirit of Christ, more then hee knowes already unlesse it be in some circumstances.

In other words, the minister and the church were no longer needed, "unlesse it be in some circumstances," since God, according to Mrs. Hutchinson, preferred to deal with His children directly.

In the same way she would have done away with the state as it then existed. Her view might have been compatible with a state concerned only with secular ends, but to the Puritans such a state would have seemed a sorry affair. Their community was a spiritual association devoted primarily to spiritual ends; and it found its laws in the general principles deducible from the Bible and from a rational observation of God's governance of the world. Her insistence on revelation apart from the Word as the source of truth had the corollary "that the will of God in the Word, or directions thereof, are not the rule whereunto Christians are bound to conforme themselves, to live thereafter." Therefore the laws which the Puritan state was enforcing could have no divine validity for her. If the state were to exist, it would have to be simply as a secular association; and that was a concept which the Puritan mind could not entertain.

These results of Mrs. Hutchinson's doctrines became apparent before the members of the orthodox group knew for certain what those doctrines were, for Mrs. Hutchinson had carefully refrained from committing herself in public. It was clear to the magistrates of the Bay Colony, however, that the nub of her teaching must consist in the idea of personal revelation, and that its consequences were at war with the ideals of Massachusetts. Because the Puritans had undergone great hardships in order to put those ideals into practice, it was only to be expected that they should do their utmost to maintain them. This we of to-day can readily understand. What is more difficult for us to comprehend is that the Puritans did not regard Mrs. Hutchinson's attack on their ideals as a difference of opinion. Miss Augur is correct is stating that Winthrop "could not recognize in Anne Hutchinson's teachings the outlines of another religious and political philosophy with its own right to exist." To concede that would have been to acknowledge that his own political and religious philosophy was wrong, and such a notion never entered his head. He could not regard the case as that of one opinion against another; it was personal opinion against truth. And the terrifying fact was that this personal opinion was gaining ground; the Word of God was being undermined by a woman. Winthrop saw the commonwealth which he had done much to found—which had been consecrated to absolute truth—rocked to its foundations by the seductive teachings of a clever lady. He could not help regarding that woman as an enemy of God. As governor he was bound to do his utmost to protect the Word and the state from this instrument of Satan.

To appreciate Winthrop's sense of responsibility it is necessary to recall the Puritans' conception of the magistrate's office. This requires an examination of that classic of Protestant political theory, the *Vindicae Contra Tyrannos*. Here we find the origin of the state described in these terms:

> Now we read of two sorts of covenants at the inaugurating of kings, the first between God, the king, and the people, that the people might be the people of God. The second, between the king and the people, that the people shall obey faithfully, and the king command justly.

The *Vindicae* explains that in these covenants "kings swear as vassals to observe the law of God, and subjects promise to obey them within the limits thus set.

From numerous statements of the Puritans it is clear that the theories of government outlined in the *Vindiciae* were those followed in Massachusetts. Although the foundation of the government was the charter from the king, all who came into the community were by tacit assumption regarded as "bound by soleme covenant to walke by the rule of Gods word in all their conversation."

• • •

That the compact was not merely between the people themselves and the magistrates whom they set up, but also between the people, the magistrates and God, is indicated by the language in which the Puritans spoke of themselves. Always they were the "People of God," and frequently they referred to their commonwealth as Israel. Furthermore, they believed the consequences of their compact to be those specified by the author of the *Vindiciae*. The latter pointed out that according to the compact, "the king himself, and all the people should be careful to honour and serve God according to His will revealed in His work, which, if they performed, God would assist and preserve their estates: as in doing the contrary, he would abandon, and exterminate them." In like manner the Puritan ministers explained to the people of New Egnland that they were a chosen people and could not "sin at so cheap a rate, or expect so few stripes for their disobedience" as those who had no covenant with the Almighty:

> Whilst a covenant people carry it so as not to break covenant, the Lord blesseth them visibly, but if they degenerate, then blessings are removed and woful Judgments come in their room.

So, while the Puritans were submissive and obedient to God—that is, so long as they submitted to His will as expressed in the Word—He would prosper all their affairs. But if they strayed and fell to open sin, He would let loose His wrath upon them.

• • •

The implications of this theory are numerous. Probably the most important is the doctrine that subjects must rebel when the magistrates command something contrary to the Law of God. More to the point in the present nstance, however, is the notion that f the ruler does not punish outward reaches of that law, the whole people nay suffer punishment at the hands of the Almighty Himself.

• • •

No one was more thoroughly imued with this socio-religious theory of criminology than Governor Winhrop. At the outset of the Bay Colony experiment, he had advised his fellow immigrants that "the care of the publique must over-sway all private respects." Later, in his controversy with young Henry Vane, Winthrop reminded the colonists that the nature of their incorporation "tyes every member thereof to seeke out and entertaine all means that may conduce to the wellfare of the bodye, and to keepe off whatsoever doth appeare to tend to theire damage." Granted this, it was the social obligation of every member of the commonwealth to refrain from breaking the Lord's commandments, for by such a breach he might bring down the divine wrath on the whole community. And it was, of course, the duty of the magistrate to protect the community by punishing the individual sinner, lest the community appear to condone sin. As Winthrop put it, "better it is some member should suffer the evill they bring upon themselves, than that, by indulgence towards them, the whole familye of God in this countrey should be scattered, if not destroyed."

It was with these beliefs in mind that the magistrates of Massachusetts began the trial of Mrs. Hutchinson. There were undoubtedly numerous personal animosities that led to the inauguration of the prosecution—the pique of the ministers and the jealousy of the magistrates. Theoretically, however, the trial was based on the charge that Mistress Hutchinson had broken the Law of God. Now it must be re-

membered that before her trial this wise woman had never publicly advanced her tenet of personal revelation. Neither had she openly professed any doctrines that could be sanely regarded as contrary to the Law of God. It was clear, nevertheless, that some one must have been urging such views privately, for the synod of ministers had found eighty-two of them to condemn. It was common rumor that that some one was Mrs. Hutchinson. Accordingly in October, 1637, she was summoned before the General Court to answer the scanty list of charges that the magistrates had been able to draw up.

• • •

The ground of the first specification was that in entertaining those who had been subsequently convicted of sedition, she had broken the fifth commandment: she had dishonored the governors, who were the fathers of the commonwealth. Her nimble wit soon put her judges in a dilemma.

> *Mrs. H.*   But put the case Sir that I do fear the Lord and my parents, may not I entertain them that fear the Lord because my parents will not give me leave?

After attempting to find his way around this logical impasse, Governor Winthrop, good Puritan casuist though he was, was forced to take refuge in dogmatic assertion.

> *Gov.*   We do not mean to discourse with those of your sex but only this; you do adhere unto them and do endeavor to set forward this faction and so you do dishonour us.

The court next called upon her to justify the weekly meetings which she held at her house. In answer she quoted two passages of Scripture: Titus II, 3-5, which indicates that the elder women should instruct the younger, and Acts XVIII, 26, wherein *"Aquila* and *Priscilla* tooke upon them to instruct *Apollo,* more perfectly, yet he was a man of good parts, but they being better instructed might teach him."

• • •

Again, after some further argument, Winthrop resorted to bare assertion, enunciating once more the Puritan theory of criminology:

. . . we see no rule of God for this, we see not-that any should have authority to set up any other exercises besides what authority hath already set up and so what hurt comes of this you will be guilty of and we for suffering you.

Undaunted by the failure to prove the first two counts, the court now moved to the final and most serious accusation, that she had insulted the ministers. The basis of this charge lay in a conference held the preceding December between the ministers and Mrs. Hutchinson. In spite of the fact that the conference had been private, the ministers now testified that she had designated them all, except Mr. Cotton and Mr. Wheelwright, as laboring under a covenant of works. The Puritan ministers were still filled with the zeal of the Reformation, and no epithet could have been better designed to arouse their ire than the one which they now declared that she had applied to them. When the court adjourned for the day, she was facing her most difficult problem.

That night she went over some notes taken at the December conference by her opponent Mr. Wilson, pastor of the Boston church. Finding that the ministers' testimonies against her were inaccurate, she demanded, when the trial reopened the following morning, that the ministers be made to give their evidence under oath. This created a

great stir and only served to strengthen the hard feeling of the court against her. Finally, however, John Cotton, teacher of the Boston church and most respected theologian of the colony, was called upon to give his version of the conference. With careful diplomacy he soother the injured pride of the other ministers and brought his speech to a dramatic close by declaring: "I must say that I did not find her saying they were under a covenant of works, nor that she said they did preach a covenant of works." And though pressed by the other ministers, he firmly stood his ground.

With this testimony the case against Mrs. Hutchinson was about to collapse. The first two specifications against her had been too weakly sustained to warrant any grave condemnation, and now the revered Mr. Cotton had practically destroyed the basis of the only remaining charge. Her triumph was too much for her. Hitherto she had been on guard and had dexterously parried every rude thrust of her prosecutors. Had she been content to hold her tongue at this point, her judges might have felt obliged to dismiss the case for lack of evidence, or at best would have passed some vote of censure in order to save their faces. Instead of continuing to rely on her native wit, she proceeded to justify herself by an immediate divine revelation.

Her prosecutors could not have hoped for a better ground upon which to condemn her. The surviving descriptions of the trial make it clear that the men who were at the same time her prosecutors and her judges had determined her guilt in advance and were merely searching for sufficient evidence on which to convict her. She herself gave them that evidence. By claiming an immediate revelation, she denied the fundamental tenet upon which the Puritan state was founded: that the Will of God was expressed directly only in the Word. Now all the previous charges could be dropped and her conviction based on this alone.

• • •

Thus ended the trial of Anne Hutchinson, a proceeding that scarcely deserves to be dignified by that name. Our indignation at its unfairness is commendable; for members of a modern state founded on self-government should be acutely conscious of the value of the forms of justice. We should remember, however, that this proceeding took place in an infant community the leaders of which looked on democracy as the worst form of government. This in no way excuses the unfairness of the trial, but it does make it easier to recognize the appropriateness of the sentence. Granted that Mrs. Hutchinson proclaimed a belief in immediate revelation, it was quite impossible that she should have been retained in the Puritan commonwealth. That our natural sympathies lie with her, rather than with the rulers of the colony, is simply an indication that the Puritan experiment failed. It was because her opinions were repellant to them that the Puritans banished Anne Hutchinson, but they sincerely believed that in thus protecting themselves they were also protecting God's eternal truth. Winthrop summed up the case in characteristic fashion, with words that have the ring of genuine feeling:

Thus it pleased the Lord to heare the prayers of his afflicted people (whose soules had wept in secret, for the reproach which was cast upon the Churches of the Lord Jesus in this Countrey, by occasion of the divisions which were grown amongst us, through the vanity of some weake minds, which cannot seriously affect any thing long, except it bee offered them under some renewed shape) and by the care and indevour of the wise and faithfull Ministers of the Churches, assisted by the Civill authority, to discover this Master-piece of the old Serpent, and to break the brood by scattering the Leaders, under whose conduct hee had prepared such Ambushment, as in all reason would soon have driven Christ and Gospel out of *New England*, (though to the ruine of the instruments themselves, as well as others) and to the repossessing of Satan in his ancient Kingdom; It is the Lords work, and it is marvellous in our eyes.

Previous selections have examined what Anne Hutchinson believed and why her ideas posed the type of threat to the Bay Colony that seemed to demand government action. In this chapter from *Fair Trial* Richard B. Morris assesses the judicial process employed against her. Morris, a noted colonial historian, has been one of the pioneers of American legal history. While he points out the inequities of Anne's trial from a modern viewpoint, he is also careful to examine it in the light of seventeenth century English judicial standards and guarantees.

RICHARD B. MORRIS

"Jezebel Before the Judges"

It could have been today instead of 1637. Allowing for differences in political climate, the sedition trial of Anne Hutchinson before her judges at Cambridge could have been staged at Foley Square, New York, . . . But Anne Hutchinson would have had a different sort of trial. The accused would still have no guarantee that her judges would judge her dispassionately, or that the jury would be uninfluenced by the inflammatory outpourings of the press. She could still not be certain that her prosecutor would not seek political advantage from her conviction. Nonetheless, she would be shielded against prejudice and hysteria to a degree unknown among the Puritan theocrats. She would be presumed innocent up to the moment when by the unanimous verdict of a trial jury she might be convicted on evidence establishing her guilt beyond a reasonable doubt. The bulwarks constructed over the course of the past three hundred years for the protection of the innocently accused would safeguard her rights.

By our standards, Anne Hutchinson did not get a fair trial in 1637. She might today.

During times of acute political tenion orthodoxy becomes a test of loyalty. People who have heterodox ideas and try to do something about them find themselves in jeopardy. People like Anne Hutchinson. It is then that the courts rouse themselves to determine the point at which ideas translated into action become an imminent danger to the state. In totalitarian states people who openly attack the leaders and foment a political opposition are liquidated out of hand or accorded the kind of trial designed to serve as a sounding-board for the state's propaganda machine. Anne Hutchinson's trial much more closely resembled a typical political trial conducted behind the iron curtain than the sort of judicial proceeding we now have a right to expect in our own country.

• • •

Whether it was the royal government trying Raleigh, or the Puritans when in power bringing the royalists to justice, the political trials of that era were partisan affairs that would outrage our sense of fair play. Furthermore, it must be remembered that in seventeenth-century England the rules of criminal procedure and evidence were still in formation. In Massachusetts, a frontier colony less than a decade old, these rules were still more elementary. Moreover, the Massachusetts Puritans, never too cordial toward the technicalities of the English common law, looked toward the Bible for instruction in criminal matters. Even John Cotton, considered a Hutchinsonian at this time, had declared: "The more any law smells of man the more unprofitable" it is. Such theocratic views could be handy weapons for leaders engaged in a fight to maintain their arbitrary power undiminished.

From the start of Anne Hutchinson's trial certain procedural safeguards

were ignored which we now consider fundamental. The prisoner was brought to trial without indictment or information, without being informed of the precise charges against her, and without even knowing what the penalty was. Since no lawyer was as yet practicing in the colony, the denial of counsel to the accused was less prejudicial in fact than it seemed on its face. But the denial of jury trial seems far more shocking. Only a year before, John Cotton had drafted a code of laws in which he did not provide for trial by jury because it was unknown in the Bible; but the authorities, regardless of their conservatism, felt this was going too far, and failed to adopt his draft. Within four years after the Hutchinson trial the colony's first written code of laws impliedly recognized jury trial and allowed the accused in criminal cases the right to elect to be tried by bench or jury.

• • •

By present-day standards of judicial propriety, John Winthrop, who presided over the tribunal, should have disqualified himself, as he was the prisoner's bitterest foe among the laity. Curiously, Winthrop was generally magnanimous, but in the Hutchinson affair he assumed the dual role of judge and prosecutor with unaccustomed relish. While normally poised and dignified on other occasions, at this time he treated the spectators to frequent unjudicial outbursts of rancor and exasperation. Had Winthrop needed a model for his behavior, he might well have chosen that Puritan hero Sir Edward Coke, who went to untoward lengths in badgering and reviling Sir Walter Raleigh when that talented Elizabethan was tried for treason. The fact is that Winthrop's conduct conformed to the accepted behavior of judges and prosecutors in English state trials. A man who believed that democracy was "the meanest and worst of all forms of government" and that the only liberty which should be tolerated was that "exercised in a way of subjection to authority" could be counted on to bring the full power of the oligarchy to bear upon dissenters, whether political or religious. "The eyes of all people are upon us," Winthrop had once counseled the settlers. "If we shall deal falsely with our God in this work we have undertaken, we shall be made a story and a byword through the world." This was a major test, and Winthrop had no intention of letting the Lord down.

Had Anne Hutchinson nurtured any hope of receiving charitable treatment at the hands of her judges, it must have been quickly dissipated when she saw Winthrop flanked by his old political rival, Thomas Dudley, the Deputy Governor, on one side, and by John Endecott on the other. When Dudley died, some verses were found in his pocket which revealed that his bigotry remained pure and uncorrupted.

Let me of God and churches watch
O'er such as do a toleration hatch,

the Deputy Governor warned, and for his epitaph chose: "I died no libertine." The grim-visaged Endecott appeared even more fanatical in his black skullcap. His tight mouth and massive jaw, only partly concealed by a gracefully pointed beard, were double assurance that these proceedings would be carried out to a suitable conclusion. The man who cut down Morton's maypole would never brook defiance of the Bible Commonwealth.

Before her judges stood the prisoner, a woman in her late forties, bereft of counsel, as was the fashion of the time. Although she was in an advanced state of pregnancy, she was forced to remain standing. Only when "her countenance discovered some bodily infirmity" was she finally permitted to sit down.

•••

The wrangling was at last interrupted by the lateness of the hour. "Mrs. Hutchinson," Winthrop declared, his patience fast ebbing, "the court you see hath labored to bring you to acknowledge the error of your way that so you might be reduced. The time now grows late. We shall therefore give you a little more time to consider of it and therefore desire that you attend the court again in the morning."

The first day had gone very well for the prisoner. She had outfenced the magistrates in a battle of wits and forced the ministers into the unchristianlike stand of having publicly revealed a private and confidential conversation. Had she had the benefit of counsel learned in the law, a nice legal question might have been raised in her behalf. Although the common-law decisions of the period were indecisive, a clever lawyer might have made a good case for the position that in English law confessions to ecclesiastics were privileged communications. Of course, Mistress Hutchinson's statements to the ministers had been more in the nature of a confidential communication than a confession according to church law, and in view of the temper of the bench it is obvious that her objection would most certainly have been dismissed on technical grounds, if no others were ready to hand. But on the moral issue Mistress Hutchinson had come off with flying colors.

The Boston bluestocking's resourcefulness had not yet been fully tested. Hardly had Winthrop convened the court the next morning when Mistress Hutchinson dropped a bombshell.

During the night, she declared she had looked over certain notes of the conference that had been taken by the Reverend Mr. Wilson. This was Vane's copy, which that disappointed young statesman had turned over to his friend before sailing for home. "I find things not to be as hath been alleged," she charged. As "the ministers came in their own cause," they should be forced to take an oath. While Winthrop insisted that since this was not a jury trial the court had full discretion in the matter of the oaths of witnesses, Bradstreet piously implored Mistress Hutchinson that, had the ministers been in error in reporting her remarks, "you would make them to sin if you urge them to swear." But the prisoner was unmoved by this plea, and many members of the court supported her.

"An oath, sir," she exclaimed to Stoughton, "is an end of all strife, and it is God's ordinance."

Sneeringly Endecott broke in: "You lifted up your eyes as if you took God to witness you came to entrap none—and yet you will have them swear!"

A hurried conference took place on the bench. Finally, in a face-saving concession, Winthrop ruled: "I see no necessity of an oath in this thing, seeing it is true and the substance of the matter confirmed by divers, yet that all may be satisfied, if the elders will take an oath they shall have it given them." Even now the court hesitated to humiliate the ministers by refusing to admit their unsworn word. "Mark what a flourish Mrs. Hutchinson puts upon the business that she had witnesses to disprove what was said, and here is no man to bear witness," the Deputy Governor broke in sarcastically.

She replied with dignity: "If you will not call them in that is nothing to me."

•••

Both sides now readied themselves for the defense's star witness, the Reverend John Cotton, who in a way was as much on trial as the prisoner. In answer to Winthrop's summons he rose from a seat beside the prisoner. As he proceeded to give his own version of the conference, he must have seemed to the spectators like a tightrope walker crossing a yawning chasm on a swaying wire—a thrill which, like the theater, their Puritan piety forbade them from enjoying. A forthright refutation of the ministers' accusation would have earned him the lasting enmity of his envious and less gifted colleagues. But should he repudiate Mistress Hutchinson's touching advocacy and devotion, he would destroy his reputation for loyalty and integrity. The course he pursued was a blend of courage and tact.

In recalling the disputed passages between Mistress Hutchinson and the pastors, Cotton admitted that he was exceedingly uncomfortable that "any comparison should be between me and my brethren." When pressed to describe the differences as the prisoner had analyzed them, he testified that she had pointed out that he "preaches the seal of the spirit upon free grace and you upon a work." These points, to Cotton's way of thinking, did not seem "so ill taken" as they are now represented. "I must say," he added, "That I did not find her saying they were under a covenant of works, nor that she said they did preach a covenant of works."

As to the issue of their competence, the Deputy Governor asked the witness: "They affirm that Mrs. Hutchinson did say they were not able ministers of the New Testament."

"I do not remember it," Cotton replied.

The learned divine's soft answers

and his conciliatory but firm testimony added up to a serious modification of the black-and-white version of the conference insisted on by the elders. Everyone present felt that a turning-point had been reached at the trial. Had the defense now rested, the Gover-ner and his supporters would have been in an extremely awkward position.

But Mistress Hutchinson's impul-siveness was to take a great load off the consciences of the magistrates. Like other women before her, she insisted on having the last word, and her rashness proved a fatal error. When Cotton took his seat, she asked the court for "leave" to "give you the ground of what I know to be true." Recklessly she plunged ahead. "The Lord knows that I could not open Scripture," she asserted. "He must by his prophetical office open it unto me." Then, more boldly, she added: "Now if you do condemn me for speaking what in my conscience I know to be truth, I must commit myself unto the Lord."

Mr. Nowell: How do you know that that was the spirit?

Mrs. H.: How did Abraham know that it was God that bid him offer his son, being a breach of the sixth commandment?

Dudley: By an immediate voice.

Mrs. H.: So to me by an immediate revelation.

At this point the Deputy Governor sneered: "How! An immediate revela-tion!" Patiently Anne Hutchinson insisted that the Lord, through the medium of the Bible, had shown her the way; Isaiah and Daniel were cited in her support. Fortified by her faith, she shouted defiantly:

"Therefore I desire you to look to it, for you see this Scripture fulfilled this day and therefore I desire you that as you tender the Lord and the church and commonwealth to con-sider and look what you do. You have power over my body, but the Lord Jesus hath power over my body and soul, and assure yourselves thus much, you do as much as in you lies to put the Lord Jesus Christ from you, and, if you go on in this course you begin, you will bring a curse upon you and your posterity, and the mouth of the Lord hath spoken it."

Another version of the trial has Mis-tress Hutchinson warning the magis-trates and elders: "Take heed how you proceed against me, for I know that for this you go about to do to me, God will ruin you and your posterity, and this whole state!"

For a moment the courtroom was stunned. So the ancient Hebrews in the synagogue of Nazareth must have reacted when they heard from the mouth of young Jesus doctrines that seemed blasphemous to their ears. No man standing on the soil of Massa-chusetts Bay had ever gone that far. Neither the ribald and profane Morton of Merrymount nor the eloquent and forthright Roger Williams had ever dared to invoke a curse upon the elders of the New Zion. Mistress Hutchinson's few rash words had en-tirely undone the effect of her own witnesses' testimony. Her judges had successfully baited her, and now they sought to spring the trap.

Winthrop: Daniel was delivered by a miracle. Do you think to be delivered so, too?

Mrs. H.: I do here speak it before the court. I look that the Lord should deliver me by his providence.

Mr. Harkalenden: I may read Scrip-ture and the most glorious hypocrite may read them and yet go down to hell.

Mrs. H.: It may be so.

• • •

The court was ready to proceed to sentencing when Deputy Brown urged that a more severe punishment be meted out to the prisoner than that which had already been imposed on her disciples, "for this is the foundation of all mischief and of all those bastardly things which have been overthrowing by that great meeting. They have all come out from this cursed fountain." Winthrop was about to put the motion for sentence when Coddington rose to his feet and made a last effort in behalf of the prisoner.

"I do not see any clear witness against her," he pointed out, "and you know it is a rule of the court that no man may be a judge and an accuser too. I would entreat you to consider whether those things which you have alleged against her deserve such censure as you are about to pass, be it to banishment or imprisonment," he continued. "I beseech you do not speak so as to force things along, for I do not for my own part see any equity in the court in all your proceedings. Here is no law of God that she hath broken nor any law of the country that she hath broke, and therefore deserves no censure."

Coddington had courageously raised fundamental issues only to be rudely handled by the Deputy Governor, who observed: "We shall be all sick with fasting." But the opposition would not be stampeded by their stomachs. Colburn openly dissented "from censure of banishment," and even the Deputy Governor refused formally to condemn Anne Hutchinson on the technical ground that the witnesses against her had not testified under oath. To "end all scruples," Winthrop ordered the elders to be sworn. There was a whispered consultation among the divines. The Reverend Messrs. Weld, Eliot, and Peters held up their hands. The Governor turned to them and put the oath: "You shall swear to the truth and nothing but the truth as far as you know. So help you God."

Anne Hutchinson's strategy had now badly backfired, for her insistence that the ministers be put to the oath merely gave them the opportunity of repeating their testimony in court for a second time and impressing it on the spectators all the more vividly. The Reverend John Eliot, some day to be renowned as the Apostle to the Indians, was most explicit in his testimony, while the other two pastors hedged somewhat.

• • •

In all, the trial consumed but two days as contrasted with major criminal trials today, which are seldom terminated under six weeks and not infrequently run on for many months. In sentencing Anne Hutchinson to deportation the authorities were invoking a penalty employed promiscuously against serious offenders as well as paupers and vagrants. Even strangers who were so indiscreet as to come to the Bay Colony leaving their wives behind in the old country would be summarily expelled.

The condemnation of Anne Hutchinson spurred the decision to liquidate the entire opposition party. At the time of Wheelwright's conviction some sixty leading Bostonians had signed a petition denying that Wheelwright had "stirred up sedition in us." Though the tone of their remonstrance was temperate, the signers were neither forgiven nor forgotten. Leading Hutchinsonians—including Coddington and Coggeshall, who had dared to speak up for the accused at the trial—were given three months to leave the colony; others were disfranchised. Charging that "there is just cause of suspicion" that the Hutchinsonians, "as others in Germany, in former times, may, upon

some revelation, make sudden erup-
tion upon those that differ from them
in judgment," the court ordered some
fifty-eight citizens of Boston and
seventeen from adjacent towns to be
disarmed unless they repudiated the
"seditious libel," by which term their
petition was now stigmatized. Winthrop recounts that some of the "chief
military officers" whose loyalties
were suspect were now forced into
line, but Captain John Underhill, the
bawdy military stalwart, remained
obdurate and had to be banished. If
any plot had sprouted, it was nipped
in the bud. As Winthrop felicitously
puts it, "when they saw no remedy,
they obeyed."

• • •

Even when she was banished from
the commonwealth and had made her
new home in Rhode Island, Anne's
enemies still pursued her. With amazing
impudence the Bay Colony authorities
sent four laymen down to Anne's
settlement to convince her of her
errors. She made short shrift of them
As soon as they announced that they
had come from Boston, she shouted
bitterly: "What from the Church at
Boston?   I know no such church,
neither will I own it. Call it the whore
and strumpet of Boston, no Church of
Christ!" Sprayed by this picturesque
Biblical buckshot, her visitors scam-
pered for cover.

But Anne and her brood continued
to be wanderers. After her husband's
death she settled at Pelham Bay, then
in Dutch New Netherland, where in
1643 she and most of her family
were treacherously murdered by
Indians. A divine judgment, the Puritan
elders called it, scarcely able to conceal
their jubilation at the news that this
Jezebel, their greatest foe, could no
longer oppose them, at least on this
earth.

Trials serve different functions. In the preceding selection
Richard B. Morris indicated that the proceedings against
Anne Hutchinson were, in effect, a political trial designed
to publicize and punish the errors of the defendant rather
than to assess her guilt or innocence. This notion is the
central theme in the following article by Anne Fairfax
Withington and Jack Schwartz. They place the proceedings
in the context of such judicial showtrials and offer new insight into the behavior of Anne Hutchinson and her judges
by interpreting their actions from that perspective.

ANNE F. WITHINGTON
and
JACK SCHWARTZ

"The Political Trial"

In November, 1637, Governor John
Winthrop opened the trial of Anne
Hutchinson. Having charged her with
disturbing the peace of the commonwealth, slandering the ministers, and
holding private meetings, he continued,
"therefore we have thought good to
send for you to understand how things
are, that if you be in an erroneous
way we may reduce you that so you
may become a profitable member
here among us, otherwise if you be
obstinate in your course that then
the court may take such course that
you may trouble us no further. . . ."

To eliminate this unprofitable member of society, the governors of the
commonwealth conducted a trial
that was as much political as it was
judicial or religious. The transcript
demonstrates the state's use of the
form of a trial as an instrument of
power to rid itself of a rebel whose
religious beliefs were threatening
the stability of the state.

• • •

Anne Hutchinson and her adherents
were accused by their opponents of
being Antinomians. . . . What distin-
quished the Boston Antinomians, if

we may believe their opponents, was the belief that a man's behavior on earth offered no clue to his fate after death. While most New England Puritans felt that once a person received grace (was "justified"), he would begin to lead a holy and righteous life (be "sanctified"), the Antinomians allegedly insisted that good conduct was no sign of salvation and bad conduct no sign of damnation— that "good" and "bad" were meaningless terms to apply to human behavior.

In a polity where social order was thought by the leaders to depend upon religious orthodoxy, Antinomianism was understandably perceived as sedition. The General Court reacted vigorously, justifying its action with biblical precedents. "...as *Cain, Hagar,* and *Ismael,* were expelled as troublers of the families, (which were then as commonwealths) so justice requires, and the necessity of the peace cals for it, that such disturbers should be put out from among us, seeing it is one of their tenents, that it is not possible their opinions, and externall peace, can stand together; and that the difference betweene them and us is (as they say) as wide as between Heaven and Hell."

• • •

In fact, however, Hutchinson cannot be proved right or wrong, nor can the state. The case of the governors of Massachusetts Bay Colony versus Hutchinson was not a case in which the rightness of one side proved the wrongness of the other. Hutchinson was not proved wrong by any standard or any law that can be applied by judicial process. She was wrong only in the terms of the state. The trial was not a trial of justice to solve the problem of guilt or innocence, but a trial of power to solve the political problem of maintaining social order.

In a sense political trials are both time-bound and timeless. Although the trial of Hutchinson as a religious dissenter who had disrupted the Massachusetts Bay commonwealth is a historical event, as a trial of a resister it is archetypal. Particular laws reflect their historical context, just as the kinds of issues that come to trial differ at different times in history. Dissent from the state will manifest itself differently in sixteenth-century England, seventeenth-century Massachusetts, and twentieth-century America. But the form of the state response —the drama in which the defendant must answer to the law for his defiance —is strikingly consistent, regardless of the historical period or the nature of the state. While the terms of the debate at trial will reflect the state's dogma, the moral drama inheres in the *fact* of the defendant's resistance, whatever its religious or ideological basis. Sir Thomas More was prosecuted for his belief in papal supremacy, Anne Hutchinson for her belief in the futility of good works, Eugene Debs for his belief in socialism and his opposition to the First World War. The beliefs were quite different but the trials were similar. For all its particular theological content, which cannot be considered without reference to Puritan modes of thought, the trial of Anne Hutchinson should be understood as an instance of the timeless form of state response to resistance— the political trial. Antigone, Thomas More, and Anne Hutchinson have a generic similarity, as do Creon, Henry VIII, and Winthrop. Hence, perhaps, the fascination which Hutchinson's trial has held for so many generations of historians.

The trial, though conducted within the context of the Puritan experiment in seventeenth-century New England, instances the general political phenom-

:non of the trial used by the state as
1 cleansing ritual for power. There is
1ever any doubt of the outcome of a
political trial—the resister will certain-
y be condemned if he does not first
submit—but the trial absolves the state
of any guilt for his elimination. The
state may use a trial to confront a
resister with his doctrinal folly, to
enmesh him in leeching formalities,
to extort that most conclusive of
tributes to power—abnegation. If the
resister does submit, obviating the
need for extirpative punishment, the
state may claim to have acted with
merciful forbearance. If the resister
does not submit, his obstinacy is
further proof of his guilt and the state
may claim the sanction of justice. In
either event the process of trial, by
providing a ritual for obscuring the
crude application of power, sustains
the moral equilibrium of political
authority.

Clothing power with law can also
hold dangers for the state. The rules
of law must be respected by the state,
at least up to a point, or else the sanctifying ritual would be worthless,
either as propaganda or self-delusion.
The state's burden to produce evidence
of the defendant's guilt, even when
the defendant is not guilty, gives the
defendant a means of striking back at
the state. If the state has a legally weak
case, a skillful defendant may humiliate the prosecution; the politically
essential condemnation at the trial's
end will then seem all the more des-
potic, and the gauze of legality the
more transparent. Another defendant,
seeing in the law only the state's
smoother tyranny, may vault over
legalisms and illuminate the real issues
by seizing the trial as a forum for self-
expression. Anne Hutchinson, remark-
ably, did both.

During the first day and a half of
her trial, Hutchinson proved herself to

be an extremely adept advocate, far
more so than her prosecutors with all
their combined strength. If the state
was going to use the law to sanctify its
proceedings against the Antinomians,
she would use the law to expose the
state. When Winthrop opened the trial
by trying to get Hutchinson to confess her errors, she immediately seized
upon the legal ritual to transform a
formal confession into a genuine evi-
dentiary hearing. "I am called here to
answer before you but I hear no things
laid to my charge." Although Winthrop
later said, "we do not call you to teach
the court but to lay open yourself,"
he could hardly disregard the legal
sanctifications; but because Hutchinson had been careful to avoid public
or written defiance, Winthrop's indictment was shaky. He first charged
her with harboring and countenancing
those of whom the magistrates dis-
approved, thereby dishonoring the
fathers of the commonwealth and thus
breaking the Fifth Commandment.
Hutchinson answered this charge with
a question: if she fears her parents and
the Lord may she not entertain those
who fear the Lord even though her
parents forbid her? Exasperated,
Winthrop could answer only, "we do
not mean to discourse with those of
your sex." Winthrop then shifted his
ground to a second charge, that Hutchinson's meetings were illegal, but this
charge also came to nothing since
Hutchinson was at least as adept as her
accusers at finding relevant scriptural
passages to substantiate a position.
With regard to recognizing the illegality
of the meetings, therefore, Winthrop
was at length driven to remind Hutchinson: "We are your judges, and not
you ours and we must compel you to
it." Hutchinson, having forced the
magistrates to settle the question by
relying on their own authority rather
than on the authority of scripture or

of law, then proceeded to bog down the court in the difficult problem of proving whether her exact words in a private meeting with some ministers of the colony eleven months before the trial were seditious heresy.

Although the unsworn evidence of the ministers built up a case against Hutchinson, she persisted in using the law as a weapon against her prosecutors. At the start of the second day's proceedings, she regained the legal offensive by demanding an oath of the ministers. Puritans believed that if they swore to anything that was false they were guilty not only of perjury but of blasphemy and would therefore be damning themselves irrevocably. By employing a procedural device of great religious import, Hutchinson threw her accusers into confusion and shifted the focus away from the content of their testimony to the form of it. (The ministers did eventually swear to their testimony, but not before Hutchinson had already ensured her banishment by her announcement of immediate revelation.) Although there was never any doubt concerning the decision the court would make, Hutchinson was forcing the court to scrutinize publicly the reasons that purported to justify her condemnation. Her demand that the court's justification be legal, when legal justification was impossible, exposed the court's attempt to use law as a sanctifying ritual.

After thus bettering the magistrates, Hutchinson transformed the trial by her announcement of immediate revelation. . . . The belief in immediate revelation was not among the charges (nor was it among the charges of any of the other Antinomians who were prosecuted by the state), and it was introduced into the trial not by the magistrates but by Hutchinson herself. Hutchinson's decision to claim immediate revelation gave the state just the legal justification needed to banish her.

• • •

To interpret Hutchinson's speech on immediate revelation as a mistake rather than a decision is convenient in building a case for the state, since Hutchinson becomes a fool rather than a resister. But Hutchinson was not a fool. For two years she had refrained from committing any act that would give the state legal grounds for proceeding against her. She had not signed a petition in favor of Wheelwright that served as the pretext for banishing many of her followers. She had consistently refused to give public utterance to her religious opinions. The only time she had expressed her opinions in front of those who disagreed with her was at a private confidential conference with the ministers of the colony, and it was one of the persistent themes of the trial that the ministers, in testifying against Hutchinson, were betraying a confidence. They may have felt that their duty to extirpate heresy was greater than their moral obligation to Hutchinson, but the members of the court knew that Hutchinson had been betrayed. Winthrop was quite defensive about it. The ministers, he claimed, had not drawn Hutchinson's opinions from her under the guise of friendship; she had told them her opinions for conscience' sake. It does not seem likely that a woman who had exercised such meticulous care in protecting herself for two years would publicly expound her theology in court by mistake. Indeed at one point in the first day of the trial, Winthrop expressed his exasperation at Hutchinson's skill as a legal tactician: "it is well discerned to the court that Mrs. Hutchinson can tell when to speak and when to hold her tongue . . . ," to which Hutchinson responded, "it is one thing for me to come before a public magistracy and there to speak what they would have me to speak and another when a man comes to me in a way of friendship privately there is a difference in that." Nor was Hutchinson thrown into confusion by being on trial. Her performance during the first day and a half proves that she was a clear-headed, sharp-witted antagonist capable of outmaneuvering her opponents.

Hutchinson's announcement of immediate revelation bespeaks her abandonment of the law. If this is not a blunder committed by a rash and reckless woman, then what is the explanation of such a seemingly senseless act? The historical evidence allows of no decisive explanation because of Hutchinson's silence on the subject of Antinomianism. It seems fair to assume, though, that Hutchinson must have believed many of the Antinomian heresies attributed to her by her enemies since she did not deny them outright. Not only does her refusal to deny Antinomianism suggest that she was indeed an Antinomian, but a belief in Antinomianism would explain her behavior at her trial. . . . Indeed, if Hutchinson was a thoroughgoing Antinomian, she would have shared with the nineteenth-century nihilists the beliefs that moral standards could not be justified by rational arguments and that human existence was trivial. To the governors of the colony certainly, the theology that they identified with Hutchinson had nihilistic consequences when applied to society. It is ironic, however, that Hutchinson should be called a nihilist, since the term was first applied to Atheists who, it was felt, would not be bound by any moral law and would therefore be immoral. Hutchinson may have been many things, but an Atheist was not one of them. The crucial difference between

Antinomians and nihilists is that Antimonians, while they did believe in the triviality of life, never for a moment extended this belief to encompass death. From everything Hutchinson's enemies said about her beliefs, it is apparent that she felt the insignificance of actions in this world precisely because she was committed to the certainty of salvation and damnation and to the omnipotence of God. Her belief that there could be no rational basis for morality would have been grounded in the belief in an omnipotent God who could never be brought into human terms.

Hutchinson's decision to abandon the law may have been a conscious affirmation of the triviality of all men's endeavors, her own as well as the court's. In this case, her decision, far from being the blunder of a foolish woman as some historians suggest, was a conscious decision to transform a hollow, fore-ordained legal ritual into a kind of personal theater: Hutchinson, after dominating the legal stage, realized herself through an act at once politically defiant and religiously satisfying. Unlike Thomas More, who believed that it was his duty to God to save himself if possible by his legal acumen, Hutchinson, having first proved that she could use the legal system far better than her opponents, then declared that the legal system was not worth using by expatiating on immediate revelation. From that moment, Hutchinson stopped playing the advocate. John Cotton took the role for a bit by trying to distinguish between revelations, but once Hutchinson had "confessed" the trial was over. As Winthrop said, "the case is altered." Only at this point, *after* Hutchinson had laid herself open, did Winthrop claim immediate revelation as the grounds for her banishment. His comment that the case is altered suggests that this was not his original intention, or at least that he had no evidence for this charge. Hutchinson's confession of immediate revelation, however, would justify her banishment, since people who looked for a direct call from God would not be bound to the ministry of the word or the laws of a biblical commonwealth.

If Anne Hutchinson believed that acts had no spiritual value, why did she make a religious statement that was bound to be politically self-destructive? Surely if acts had no value, it would have been better for her to continue to try to win the trial and, if not prevent her banishment, at least expose the state's use of legal ritual to disguise power. By rejecting the legal process and deciding to defy the state in her own religious terms rather than in the legal terms of the governors, Hutchinson allowed the trial to fulfill its function as a cleansing ritual. Not only did the trial itself have a cleansing effect on the politics of the time, but the transcript of the trial seems to have had a cleansing effect on the historical record. Historians have glossed over the perversion of the legal process and misinterpreted the import of Hutchinson's action.

Having made her decision to talk about immediate revelation, Hutchinson addressed the court: "Now if you do condemn me for speaking what in my conscience I know to be truth I must commit myself unto the Lord." Hutchinson, in the very process of denying the significance of human acts, seems, by grounding her decision in conscience, to be committing a spiritually significant act. No one, after all, is asking her about immediate revelation; she herself, allowing her conscience to precipitate

her into action, introduces immediate revelation. Conscience can mean different things, but it always has some connection with action. Usually conscience means the faculty that passes judgment on acts already committed. "My conscience hath a thousand several tale, / And every tale condemns me for a villain." It can also mean mental awareness of possible actions or possible consequences of action, an awareness which can sometimes stagnate action. "Thus conscience doth make cowards of us all," says Hamlet, who, although he hates life, cannot kill himself or avenge his father, because too much thinking has destroyed his resolution. But, most significantly for the case of Anne Hutchinson, conscience can be a guide to, and cause of, action. Before the Holy Roman Emperor, Christendom, and God, Martin Luther refused to recant: "I cannot and I will not recant anything, for to go against conscience is neither right nor safe. God help me. Here I stand; I can do not otherwise." This is the conscience of Anne Hutchinson. Ironically, Hutchinson, who does not believe in the significance of human acts, has a conscience that compels her to act. She does not make her decision to talk about immediate revelation because of any consequences such a speech might have, but because she feels that it is right. Even though Hutchinson may not recognize moral value, she does recognize moral obligation, not to any law, but to God himself. Her act is not good or bad, it has no significance in terms of salvation or society, but it is right because it follows conscience, the voice of God.

At the opening of Anouilh's *Antigone*, the chorus explains the difference between tragedy and melodrama. Since the outcome of tragedy is inevitable, whatever the participants say, they say not because they hope to change the course of events, but because what they say ought to be said. In melodrama people argue and struggle in the hope of escaping, which is vulgar and practical. "But in tragedy, where there is no temptation to try to escape, argument is gratuitous: it's kingly." By abandoning legal tactics and openly declaring her position on immediate revelation, Hutchinson does not change the outcome of her trial; she accepts it. Her friends have already received the sentence of banishment; she will receive the sentence of banishment. As long as she continues to participate in the legal proceedings, she is denying her own belief in the futility of human endeavor; she therefore stops arguing and delivers a "kingly," "gratuitous" speech on immediate revelation.

To say that Anne Hutchinson in publicly affirming her belief in immediate revelation accepted her political fate is not to say that she understood it. Her question to Winthrop at the end of her trial, "Wherefore am I banished?" was probably genuine. Winthrop, having achieved the objective of power with punctilious deference to the legal ritual, could reply, "say no more, the court knows wherefore and is satisfied." But Hutchinson may not have known "wherefore." Once Hutchinson had rejected the legal process, she and Winthrop were on entirely different planes and no longer able to communicate with each other. At this point Hutchinson might have said to Winthrop what Antigone said to Creon, "now it is you who have stopped understanding. I am too far away from you now, talking to you from a kingdom you can't get into, with your quick tongue and your hollow heart."

The Social Dimension

Kai Erikson is a sociologist who chose to study Puritan society because its isolation and the relatively small size of the population combined with an abundance of documentation to make it ideal for testing various hypotheses. His prime concern was to analyze the nature of deviance: how does a society agree on what is or is not criminal behavior and what effect does that process have on the society itself? Through an analysis of the Antinomian controversy, the persecution of Quakers, and the Salem witchcraft hysteria he argues that such incidents are important not only for their effect on the objects of the proceedings but also for what they say about the society. In punishing an individual such as Anne Hutchinson the community not only indicated what it would not tolerate but it made clear what it stood for.

KAI T. ERIKSON

"Wayward Puritans"

DURING the first six decades of settlement in Massachusetts, three serious "crime waves" occurred which affected the young colony in decisive ways. Each of these waves became an object of wide public concern and each of them drew large numbers of deviant offenders. In the long chapter to follow, we will look at these episodes in turn to see what impact they had on the emerging outlines of the Puritan commonwealth. The narrative will try to argue that the Antinomian controversy of 1636, the Quaker persecutions of the late 1650's, and the witchcraft hysteria of 1692 were three different attempts by the people of the Bay to clarify their position in the world as a whole, to redefine the boundaries which set New England apart as a new experiment in living.

When the New England Puritans put an entire ocean between themselves and the rest of the world, they were declaring in effect that issues of the most profound gravity divided them from their contemporaries at home. They had voyaged many miles to establish a new model of Christian fellowship, an ethic they could call the "New England Way," and it was naturally important to them that this ethic have a clear enough character to stand out from other ideologies and other programs in the world of the time. The New England Way was to represent their uniqueness as a people, their justification for withdrawing into the empty spaces of America; it was to be their history, their folklore, their special emblem, their destiny. Throughout the early years of settlement, then, as shifts in the political climate of Europe changed the background against which the colony measured its own particular character, the people of the Bay had to review again and again what qualities distinguished them from the rest of mankind. It would be quite a few years before they began to regard the land they had settled as a nation: New England was not a "place" to them but a "way," not a country but an experimental proving ground in which a new kind of religious spirit could be tested and developed. And this meant that the settlers had to be extremely thoughtful about the political and religious institutions they were building in their wilderness home, for they knew that the identifying mark of their "way" would only be seen in the architecture of their commonwealth: in the form of their government, the organization of their church, the tenor of their law.

. . .whenever a community is confronted by a significant relocation of boundaries, a shift in its territorial position, it is likely to experience a change in the kinds of behavior handled by its various agencies of control. The occasion which triggers this boundary crisis may take several forms—a realignment of power within the group, for example, or the appearance of new adversaries outside it—but in any case the crisis itself will be reflected in

altered patterns of deviation and perceived by the people of the group as something akin to what we now call a crime wave. These waves dramatize the issues at stake when a given boundary becomes blurred in the drift of passing events, and the encounters which follow between the new deviants and the older agents of control provide a forum, as it were, in which the issue can be articulated more clearly, a stage on which it can be portrayed in sharper relief.

Now this general hypothesis must be qualified in two important ways. First, when one argues that boundary crises are apt to set "crime waves" into motion, one is suggesting two things —that the community begins to censure forms of behavior which have been present in the group for some time but have never attracted any particular attention before, and that certain people in the group who have already acquired a disposition to act deviantly move into the breach and begin to test the boundary in question. For the moment it is not important to distinguish between these two sources of deviant behavior, except to point out that the severity of a "crime wave" cannot always be measured by the number of deviant offenders involved or the volume of deviance in fact committed. In the sense that the term is being used here, "crime wave" refers to a rash of publicity, a moment of excitement and alarm, a feeling that something needs to be done. It may or may not mean an actual increase in the volume of deviation.

Second, the appearance of a boundary crisis does not necessarily mean that a *new* set of boundaries has attracted attention or even that some important change has taken place within the basic structure of the community itself. Ordinarily, it only means that a different sector of the community's traditional boundary network has moved into focus and needs to be more carefully defined.

• • •

The Antinomian Controversy

The Antinomian controversy of 1636-1638 did not begin as a "crime wave" in any ordinary sense. It was a convulsive episode, a moment of restlessness which moved across the colony like a puff of wind and suddenly exploded into one of the stormiest events in a whole generation of New England history. If the men and women who provoked the crisis had been better organized and surer of their own purposes, we might remember them as founders of an important new social movement. But as it was, few of those active people really understood the significance of the theory they advanced or the violence of the storm they managed to stir up.

• • •

The main purpose of the Puritan experiment in those early days was to show that men could govern themselves in a political state exactly as they governed themselves in a church congregation—that the Bible could serve as a competent instrument of law, that sainthood could provide a feasible basis for citizenship, and that the ministers could act as the final moral authority in civil as well as spiritual matters. As the commonwealth slowly took form, the Puritan magistrates began to operate on the basis of a political theory which borrowed most of its metaphors from English Congregationalism but which represented something of a departure from at least the mood of that earlier doctrine. In its first stages, as we have seen, Puritanism can be said to have contained a strong note of individualism, if only in the sense that it appealed

directly to the individual conscience and promoted a respect for private religious expression and experience. Now this sense of individuality fit naturally into Puritan thinking so long as it was voiced by a people protesting against the authority of a Rome or a Canterbury, but when these protesters themselves moved into power and became the custodians of their own church, a rapid shift in emphasis was necessary. By virtue of one long sea voyage, the New England Puritans had been transformed from an opposition party into a ruling elite, and one of the central concerns for the Massachusetts leadership was to capture the emotional resources which had sustained the earlier protest and harness them to the needs of a tightly disciplined orthodoxy. Thus a new brand of Puritanism was taking shape in the forests of New England: the piety and self-expression which had dominated the original tone of the movement was gradually being transformed into the loyalty and obedience necessary for a civil establishment. A people who had trained themselves to police their own hearts and control their own impulses were now being asked to apply the same discipline to the community as a whole.

Whereas the early Puritan theorists had emphasized the private nature of each person's covenant with God, the New England theorists began to argue that God had entered into a covenant with the people of the colony as a corporate group and was only ready to deal with them through the agencies they had built to govern themselves. Thus the key idea of the new theology was that an individual's relationship to God needed to be screened by some intermediate level of authority—a congregation, a government, an administration. Looking back at this shift in focus from the seasoned perspective of another century, it would seem that the people of the Bay were constructing much the same kind of control apparatus they had fought against in England; but some form of external discipline was necessary if the colony were to survive at all, and few settlers seemed concerned that the earlier individualism of the movement was quietly disappearing. In theory, at least, each soul was left to negotiate his own way to heaven and was encouraged to act upon the promptings of his own conscience; but in fact, an administrative machinery was slowly developing to make sure that each private conscience was rightly informed and loyal to the policies and programs of the state. The clergy, naturally, played an important role in this arrangement. It became their job to keep order among the various congregations, to instruct men in their duty toward the state as well as toward God, and perhaps most important, to lead the congregation in deciding what persons were eligible for membership in the larger corporation. Ministers could not hold public office, nor could they interfere too actively in political affairs, but they played a leading part in determining who among the settlers had experienced a true conversion and so deserved the privileges of the franchise. In many respects, the whole structure of the New England Way rested on that one article, for the purpose of the enterprise was to prove that God's chosen saints could and should take charge of His earthly commonwealth. No one would pretend that there were any infallible guidelines for deciding who was saved and who was not, but someone had to make human judgments in the absence of divine knowledge, and this responsibility, inevitably, fell to the clergy.

As we shall see, the Antinomian controversy centered on that very point, for it was the contention of Mrs. Hutchinson and her followers that almost no ministers in the Bay were competent to judge whether a person was truly touched by grace or not, and in doing so, they were challenging one of the most important cornerstones of the whole experiment. They were saying in effect that the spirited individualism of the old movement could not be converted into the orthodoxy of the new, and they did so at a time when this difference meant all the world to the settlers of New England.

• • •

Mrs. Hutchinson's debate with the ministry of Massachusetts was conducted in such an exhausting barrage of words and ideas that the underlying shape of the quarrel is difficult to follow—particularly if we are encouraged by the tone of the argument to assume that it was theological rather than political. The historian Charles Francis Adams concluded:

> Not only were the points in dispute obscure, but the discussion was carried on in a jargon which has become unintelligible; and, from a theological point of view, it is now devoid of interest. At most, it can excite only a faint curiosity as one more example of the childish excitement over trifles by which people everywhere and at all times are liable to be swept away from the moorings of common sense.

Adam's exasperation with the text of the debate must be taken seriously, for no student has ever studied the episode more carefully. Still, the importance of the Antinomian controversy lies not so much in what was said as in the form of the events which followed. In order to understand why sensible people would brawl over such "trifles" we should look at the larger situation rather than the details of the argument itself, for the affair had a shape and a logic which were not wholly reflected in the words that were spoken.

To begin with, Mrs. Hutchinson was a woman, and this simple matter must have added appreciably to the elders' sense of irritation. Puritan notions about the role of women in community life were less than progressive even by the standards of the seventeenth century—a fact made abundantly clear by Winthrop when he explained that a woman of his acquaintance had become mentally ill as a result of reading too many books: "for," he added by way of editorial, "if she had attended her household affairs, and such things as belong to women, and not gone out of her way and calling to meddle in such things as are proper for men, she had kept her wits, and might have improved them usefully and honorably in the place that God had set her." Needless to say, men like Winthrop would have been annoyed by a woman of Mrs. Hutchinson's belligerent intelligence whether they knew what she was talking about or not.

In one respect, however, everyone knew what Mrs. Hutchinson was talking about. When she declared that only Cotton and Wheelwright among the many ministers of the Bay were "walking in a covenant of grace," with the obvious corollary that the others all preached a "covenant of works," she was touching a highly sensitive nerve in her Puritan audience. Vague as they were, these two phrases had played a prominent role in the early history of the Reformation and were still capable of stirring up old angers and insecurities.

According to the Puritan reading of Genesis, God had once promised Adam that his seed would enjoy ever-lasting life so long as he kept away from the tree of knowledge, the forbidden fruit. Adam had failed to honor that straightforward contract, of course, and mankind had been condemned to toil, hardship, and eventual death. But then God offered another covenant to man in which He agreed to save a scattering of persons from damnation in an entirely arbitrary way, drawing them at random from among His people and bestowing His grace upon them in advance. The most important feature of this new covenant was that there would be no more guarantees, no more opportunities for men to earn salvation by a display of good conduct. At its simplest, the first of these arrangements was the covenant of works, while the latter substitute was the covenant of grace.

Now these two "covenants" were essentially an invention of Reformation thinking. When the first generation of reformers challenged the authority of Rome, they argued that the formal structure of the Catholic Church—its regulations, its formulae, it alms and dispensations—were really a throwback to the forfeited covenant of works, because the Church seemed to be teaching that men could earn their way to heaven by observing a few simple rules exactly as Adam might have won salvation for all his seed by observing a single prohibition. The covenant of grace, then, had a very special meaning in this context. If salavation occurs at random and has no relation to the actual conduct of men on earth, then people do not need any religious services to prepare them for eternity or any class of priests to intercede in their behalf. Grace is an intimate exchange, a personal communication between God and His chosen saints.

Like many other tenets of Reformation thought, however, this distinction between grace and works was more often taken as a metaphor than as a literal sanction, one which might be interpreted literally by a sect struggling against an established church, but one which had to be phrased with extreme care by any party in power. In its purest form, the covenant of grace was almost an invitation to anarchy, for it encouraged people to be guided by an inner sense of urgency rather than by an outer form of discipline; if the notion were taken at face value there would be no end to the amount of mischief a person might do. Supposed someone mistook an upset stomach for a divine call and charged off to do battle with even the most legitimate authority? No, the covenant of grace might make good material for a revolutionary slogan, but it was hardly the kind of doctrine a government could afford to tolerate in its undiluted form once that government came to power. When Martin Luther first rebelled against Rome, for example, and broke his monastic vows, he justified his action on the ground that he had received a divine summons; but later, when all Germany was torn by the new doctrines and the peasants rose in what they thought was a religious crusade, he had to turn away in horror. Somehow the voices which spurred the peasants into civil war did not seem to have the same divinity as the voices which drew Luther away from the Church, and the problem for the more responsible reformers was to create an agency which could distinguish between the two without returning to the formality and discipline of the Catholic Church. Throughout the early history of the Reformation this dilemma had appeared again and again, and the people of New England were no more immune. They had confronted the Anglican bishops by arguing that each man should be free to negotiate his way to heaven without interference from a central church hierarchy, but now, with a land to settle and a people to govern, the tone of their argument was bound to change. When the Boston insurgents were called "Antinomians," the familiar cycle seemed to be repeating itself, for this was the name given to the desperate heretics of Luther's day and a name many ministers in the Bay had heard applied to themselves in old England.

Anne Hutchinson may not have been an Antinomian in the purest sense of the term, but she seemed to advocate a kind of religious enthusiasm which was simply not possible among an orthodox company of saints. She spoke to a people whose sense of theology had been sharpened by the endless controversies of the Reformation, and to them the main text of her argument was altogether clear. If saints are joined to God by a covenant of grace, she asked, why is it necessary for them to accept the discipline of an earthly church? If God bestows His grace directly on the recipient in a private moment of conversion, why should that gift be ratified by an official of the church who himself may not be chosen? It is difficult to know how far Mrs. Hutchinson meant to go in her distrust of church control, since few of her own words have survived. But she did announce that the incumbent ministers of the Bay were not fit to occupy their pulpits; and whatever else she might have thought about the role of church discipline in a community of saints, this opinion was quite enough to set the whole machinery of the state against her.

In several respects, then, Mrs. Hutchinson was only repeating an exaggerated version of what many Puritan preachers had said before, and perhaps it is true, as she claimed, that many of her ideas were drawn from the early sermons of John Cotton. But Puritan theory had been revised considerably since Cotton was a young minister in Lincolnshire. The credo of a minority group had become the platform of a ruling party, and in the process it had acquired a number of new responsibilities. Gradually, then, two amendments to the original theory of grace had worked their way into Congregational thinking, each of them representing a change in tone rather than a distinct change in doctrine. The first of these was the notion that certified ministers were competent to judge who had experienced a true conversion and who had not, giving them whatever warrant they needed to screen candidates for church membership and for the franchise. The second was the notion that even the surest saint should be subject to church discipline and governed by the will of the congregation, not because his future reward depended upon it, exactly, but because a person needs to be adequately prepared for the gift of grace when it comes. The ministers were careful to point out that these shifts in theory did not represent any return to the discredited covenant of works, but the line between the two positions became more and more difficult to see as it became apparent that one of the easiest ways for a person to convince his fellows that he was truly saved was to become a devoted servant of the church and a loyal citizen of the state. As Mrs. Hutchinson very correctly sensed, a new strain had appeared in New England thinking. The ministers were not arguing that outer conformity was necessary to *earn* salvation, but they seemed to be saying that outer conformity was a convenient way to *prove* salvation; and thus the covenant

of grace had lost so much of its inner mystery that it did bear some resemblance to the older covenant of works. The clergy were quite positive that they could explain the difference logically, but they spent so many awkward hours in this pursuit that they appeared to betray their uneasiness every time they mounted the pulpit or took their pens in hand.

The danger of Mrs. Hutchinson's position, of course, was that she did not want to give the ministers the authority they needed to use the covenant of grace as a political instrument. In the beginning, perhaps, her quarrel with the clergy was a personal matter: she was entirely confident of her own election and did not think for a moment that a preacher like Wilson, whatever his offices or degrees from Cambridge, was competent to review her qualifications for sainthood. She was quite sure that godly behavior on this earth was no evidence that one had been chosen for salvation in the next. Now all of this was according to the best Puritan usage of a generation earlier, and had she addressed her arguments to the Anglican churchmen rather than the New England divines, she might have earned a good deal of credit for her stand. But Mrs. Hutchinson did not appreciate how the world had changed. Sainthood in New England had become a political responsibility as well as a spiritual condition, and when she hinted that her election set her above the government of ordinary men she seemed to be asking for a license which no administration could safely confer. It is important to remember that Mrs. Hutchinson did not really ask for such a license, nor did she deny the jurisdiction of the government over her—but she had chosen a highly suggestive metaphor in an attempt to phrase her discontents accurately, and in doing so, had reminded these children of the Reformation about issues that had been festering under the surface for many years. It was not Mrs. Hutchinson's voice so much as her echo which started the Antinomian controversy in Massachusetts Bay.

The case against Mrs. Hutchinson and her followers, then, was largely a political one. The arguments which emerged from the Hutchinson parlor were cloaked in the language of theology, but (to the extent that the two could be distinguished in seventeenth-century thought) the charge against them was sedition rather than heresy, and once the leading men of the colony began to notice the effect Mrs. Hutchinson's crusade was producing among the settlers of the Bay, they moved heavily to the attack.

• • •

The civil trial of Anne Hutchinson took place in November, 1637, and a transcript of these proceedings has been preserved. In many respects, the trial can tell us as much about the confusions generated by the Antinomian controversy as any number of other documents, for it is our only opportunity to see the opposing forces in actual confrontation. Although a lone woman stood before the bar, in poor health and entirely without counsel, a whole way of life was on trial. Anne Hutchinson represented not only a dissatisfied group of colonists numbering over a hundred but a strain of Puritanism which the colony could no longer afford to recognize. When Governor Winthrop and Mistress Hutchinson faced each other across the bare wooden table which served as a bench, they wore the expressions of an austere magistrate and of a brash, contentious housewife; but the voices in which they spoke carried a tone of far greater significance. Mrs. Hutchinson symbolized the lively enthusiasm of the old

Puritanism while Governor Winthrop symbolized the political maturity of the new, and the dialogue which followed can hardly be appreciated unless this is kept in mind. From its opening moments, the exchange seems restless and uncertain—which should not be at all surprising, for the two principals were trying to speak a language which had not yet been invented, to argue an issue which had not yet been defined. In a sense, the trial was an attempt to develop such a language.

• • •

Modern readers often find it difficult to read the transcript of Anne Hutchinson's trial without projecting their twentieth-century sympathies into that seventeenth-century text. The proceedings were surely a cruel miscarriage of justice, even by the standards of the time, and it seems entirely natural to cast the poor defendant in a martyr's role. But this may be a misleading way to see the story, for Mrs. Hutchinson was a full partner in the transactions which led to her banishment and did as much as anyone else to set its basic tone and character. We do not know whether she got what she *wanted* from the court, of course, but it is fairly clear that she got what she *expected*, and in fact played an active role in realizing that prediction. Both sides tried to goad the other into making a declaration of their position; both hoped to establish the line which distinguished Mrs. Hutchinson's brand of Congregationalism from the more orthodox stand of the magistrates.

On the whole, then, it is easier to understand the main drift of the hearing if one forgets for the moment that it took the form of a criminal trial. The confrontation between Anne Hutchinson and the magistrates of Massachusetts was a tribal ceremony, a morality play, a ritual encounter between two traditional adversaries, and it is fair to assume that both the prosecution and the defense were more aware of the informal rules governing the occasion than any of the commentators who have studied it since. Like dancers tracing the steps of a familiar ceremony, all the participants in the drama must have known what its eventual outcome would be; but the form of the ritual had to be observed if that outcome were to have any lasting meaning. Although the trial continued for many hours, through many shifts of topic and many changes of legal posture, it never lost its relentless tone of certainty. In the end, Winthrop invited the court's verdict with almost the same phrase used by Dudley at the beginning of the proceedings: "The court hath already declared themselves satisfied concerning the things you hear, and concerning the troublesomeness of her spirit and the danger of her course among us, which is not to be suffered." And a moment later, when Mrs. Hutchinson asked the court to explain the basis of its decision, she was told flatly, "say no more, the court knows wherefore and is satisfied."

And that was exactly the point. The court *did* know why Mrs. Hutchinson had to be banished, but it did not know how to express that feeling in any language then known in New England. The settlers were experiencing a shift in ideological focus, a change in community boundaries, but they had no vocabulary to explain to themselves or anyone else what the nature of these changes were. The purpose of the trial was to invent that language, to find a name for the nameless offense which Mrs. Hutchinson had committed. All in all, Anne Hutchinson and her band of followers were guilty of something called "Hutchinsonianism," no more and no less, and

one of the main outcomes of the trial was to declare in no uncertain terms that people who acted in this fashion had trespassed the revised boundaries of the New England Way.

● ● ●

Although it is convenient to place Mrs. Hutchinson in the center of the Antinomian controversy and describe the whole affair as if it were somehow an extension of her unusual character, no amount of personal biography can explain by itself the events which led to her banishment. Our problem is not to learn why a woman of her odd opinions and leanings should appear in seventeenth-century Boston, but rather why the people of the colony should become so alarmed over the brittle philosophies she taught in her parlor. If, as Winthrop thought, she had "seduced" the good people of Boston by her crafty conceits, it was only because they were ready for that kind of diversion anyway; and thus it is far more important to understand the shifts of mood that made the settlers responsive to her arguments than to understand the manner in which she presented them. People like Mrs. Hutchinson can be found anywhere, driven to a deep excitement by the urgency of their own convictions. They become leaders of insurrections or prophets of change only when the community around them begins to listen to the words they have been repeating all along, and then they are apt to become captives of their own unexpected audience. In 1636 the townsfolk of Boston decided to join her in her lonely crusade, and in doing so placed her in the midst of a crucial historical crossroads.

This crossroads was not marked by familiar signs, for the people of the Bay were not really aware that they had reached it. Puritan theory in New England had begun to change: it had lost much of its original emphasis on individual religious experience in order to promote the newer doctrine of "preparation" for salvation, which Miller has called "the peculiar badge of New England's theology," and as a result, the whole notion of grace no longer had the same intimacy or the same revolutionary force. This was a change which could not be explained easily. Massachusetts Bay was a community which owed its origins to the idea that church and state should be separate, a community which had pioneered the decentralization of ecclesiastical authority, a community fashioned in the belief that each person was primarily responsible to the promptings of his own conscience; and in such a community there were no theories or traditions to relate what had happened to the New England Way, no vocabulary of words to explain this shift in focus. In many ways, the magistrates' decision to banish Mrs. Hutchinson was a substitute for the words they could not find. The verdict against her was a public statement about the new boundaries of Puritanism in Massachusetts Bay, for in passing sentence on Mrs. Hutchinson the magistrates were declaring in the only way they could that the historical stage she had come to represent was now past. No simpler language was available for that purpose.

Language is such a basic fact of our everyday existence that we often take it for granted. We assume that words have always played the same role in the communications process. Patricia Caldwell reminds us in this article that European society during the Reformation experienced a shift from traditional oral forms of communication in which communal consensus defined the meaning of words to a world in which the individual was learning to confront and come to terms with the written word in the form of the Scriptures. Understanding of the meaning of words no longer came from the community but from inspired reading. Applying this perspective, Caldwell contends that to some degree the controversy which Anne Hutchinson generated may have resulted from the fact that she was in effect speaking a different language.

PATRICIA CALDWELL

"The Antinomian Language Controversy"

Ever since the Boston Church cast out Anne Hutchinson in 1638, the fact of her having "made a Lye" has stood without question. But why she told "so horrible an Untruth and falshood, or what it meant to her to do so, has not always been so clear. Part of the problem is an irony so deeply imbedded in the lie itself that it almost escapes notice: when Mrs. Hutchinson denied that she had held the erroneous opinions which countless people had heard her openly proclaim, she was inadvertently saying something about the relationship between thinking and speaking—something about language itself. That "something," though neither she nor her adversaries could fully grasp or articulate it, was felt be so subversive that the mere presence of its perpetrator in the community was deemed utterly intolerable: a dishonor to Jesus Christ and a "sine agaynst God".

History has been kinder to the "Notorius Imposter", treating with detachment and even with sympathy the social, economic, political and psychological implications of her predicament. Yet the fundamental problems of language that lurk beneath the surface of her "manifest evil in matter of conversation" have still to be explored. An assortment of similar problems can be detected beneath the "immediate revelation" which Mrs. Hutchinson shockingly proclaimed during her earlier examination by the General Court. Although her behavior at the Newtown examination has been accounted for by everything from "arrogance" to an oversupply of "imagination," something puzzling still remains in the language of the documents, just as it does in the church records. Clearly, Anne Hutchinson in both of her trials was more than an out-and-out liar. What, after all, was she really saying when she made those two fateful declarations: that God had spoken to her by an immediate voice, and that her judgments had always been sound, though her expressions had not?

Long ago, Charles Francis Adams uncovered a fragment of the answer: "The real difficulty lay in the fact that the words and phrases to which they attached an all-important significance did not admit of definition, and, consequently, were devoid of exact meaning. They were simply engaged in hot wrangling over the unknowable." Adams was too impatient with the "ecclesiastical persecution" that hunted Anne Hutchinson like a "frightened fox" to pursue this possibility. But he did raise a crucial point: whatever else it may have been, the Antinomian Controversy was a monumental crisis of language. The trial documents suggest that Mrs. Hutchinson was neither purposely deceiving nor hallucinating, and that her words cannot fairly be ascribed to mere stubbornness, hysteria, personal assertiveness, nor even to a poor education. They suggest that Mrs. Hutchinson was speaking what amounts to a different language —different from that of her adversaries, different even from that of John Cotton—and that other people may have been speaking and hearing as she was, and that what happened to them all had serious literary consequences in America.

In his noted journal passage of 1636, John Winthrop set down the two "dangerous errors" that became the root theological issues in the Antinomian Controversy: "1. That the person of the Holy Ghost dwells in a justified person. 2. That no sanctification can help to evidence to us our justification." In her own defense, Mrs. Hutchinson also made two claims—and these were, in effect, statements about *language*. First, at the General Court (Mrs. Hutchinson having said that "the Lord, he hath let me see which was the clear ministry and which the wrong"):

> *Mr. Nowell.* How do you know that that was the spirit?
> *Mrs. H.* How did Abraham know that it was God that bid him offer his son, being a breach of the sixth commandment?
> *Dep. Gov.* By an immediate voice.
> *Mrs. H.* So to me by an immediate revelation.
> *Dep. Gov.* How! an immediate revelation.
> *Mrs. H.* By the voice of his own spirit to my soul.

Second, at the church trial (during an attempt to determine whether—or when—Mrs. Hutchinson denied "inherent graces" in the saints, one of the worst heresies of which she was accused):

> *Mr. Cotton.* Thear is 2 thinges to be clerd, 1. what you doe not hould. 2ly what you did hould.
> *Mrs. Hutchinson.* My Judgment is not altered though my Expression alters.

When these sets of statements—the doctrinal questions reported by Winthrop, and the claims of Mrs. Hutchinson at the trial—are held side by side, it can be seen that the latter (Hutchinson) pair is an exact linguistic analogue to the former (doctrinal) pair. Whether it is possible to determine a causal sequence—whether we can say that Mrs. Hutchinson's language emerges from her religious conceptions, or vice versa—is not certain. To decide that question would be in a sense to decide the Antinomian Controversy itself. We can at least say with Kenneth Burke that

> insofar as man is the "typically symbol-using animal," it should not be surprising that men's thoughts on the nature of the Divine embody the principles of verbalization. . . . This investigation does not require us to make any decisions about validity of theology *qua* theology. Our purpose is simply to ask how theological principles can be shown to have usable secular analogues that throw light upon the nature of language.

In this case, we are looking at the American language in its embryonic period. Since it was very largely a spiritual idiom, the "jargon" which Charles Francis Adams so swiftly dismissed is the crucial element, for the theological ideas are inseparable from the basic verbal "ideas." The first erroneous doctrine attributed to Mrs. Hutchinson—"that the person of the Holy Ghost dwells in a justified person"—corresponds to her conviction that a divine voice speaks to her soul, and to a related feeling on her part that merely human language is not to be trusted. The second doctrine—"no sanctification can help to evidence to us our justification"—coincides with Mrs. Hutchinson's insistence that expressions are no evidence of judg-

ments. In short, Mrs. Hutchinson's "errors" are not disembodied codes and dogmas, but intricate networks of sense, feeling, thought and expression. Therefore we are forced to ponder the exasperating complexities of the Antinomian Controversy not only as differences of opinion, but as differences of perception.

The first question—that of the indwelling of the Holy Spirit—stands at the center of a vast cluster of issues raised in both trials concerning the soul's union with Christ, the nature of the body and of the soul, the distinction between soul and spirit and between God's spirit and man's spirit, and the exact mechanics of resurrection. But throughout the tangled testimony, there is one point on which Mrs. Hutchinson never wavers: she consistently and relentlessly focuses on the person of Christ and on the moment of union. Her focus is so intense that she even dislodges the cardinal events of sacred history in order to superimpose them on the moment of Redemption, so that Creation is actually repeated (the created human soul is only "immortall by Redemption", and the Second Coming is now ("By Cominge of Christ . . . meanes his *cominge to us in Union*"). Christ so overwhelms Mrs. Hutchinson that she even denies the resurrection of the body, for "I cannot yet see that Christ is united to these fleshly Bodies. And if he be not. . . than those Bodies cannot rise". A midwife and mother of many children, Mrs. Hutchinson seems especially disturbed by the thought of the dead bodies lying in their graves, grimly unworthy of rising to salvation. Although her exact view of what should happen on the last day is not clear, she obviously feels a profound distrust for anything merely human, even in the face of the divine power to elevate and transform.

Mrs. Hutchison. . . . . I will propound my mayne scruple and that is *how a Thinge that is Immortally miserable can be immortally happie.*

Mr. Cotten. He that makes miserable can make us happy.

Mrs. Hutchison. I desire to hear God speak this and not man. Shew me whear thear is any Scripture to prove it that speakes soe.

According to Winthrop's *Short Story* of the Antinomian affair, Mrs. Hutchinson is supposed to have said, *"Give me Christ, I seeke not for graces, but for Christ, I seeke not for promises, but for Christ, I seeke not for sanctification, but for Christ, tell not me of meditation and duties, but tell me of Christ".* Winthrop, explicating such views, wrote, "Christ was all, did all, and. . .the soule remained alwayes as a dead Organ". Mrs. Hutchinson's single-minded insistence on Christ does seem to exclude and even to eliminate what is human, in the sense that, as Winthrop complained, "to destroy the faculties of the soule, is to destroy the immortality of the soule. . . . In stead of them, [the Antimonians hold that] the Holy Ghost doth come and take place, and doth all the works of those natures, as the faculties of the human nature of Christ do". Precisely here, on this question of the rational human faculties, Mrs. Hutchinson stands apart from her adversaries. Insofar as speech is a human faculty, she appears not to trust it in the same way that they do. Even God's contract with her is perceived not so much by actual words as "by the voice of his own spirit to my soul." Of course, there is nothing unusual in the idea of the divine voice; it is in the very fiber of Puritan thought.

• • •

But strangely, during the long "spiritual autobiography" that Mrs. Hutchinson delivers in General Court, the Deity is portrayed only once as "speaking." It is as if Mrs. Hutchinson is reluctant to conceive of God actually saying words: he shows, he reveals, he opens, he gives promises, he "let me see" and he "let me to distinguish between the voice of my beloved and the voice of Moses, the voice of John Baptist and the voice of antichrist".

• • •

Her dependence on the Bible suggests that the complaint by the ministers that Mrs. Hutchinson rejects Scripture is not strictly accurate. What is apparent is that she cannot find a point of contact between the scriptural words of those men who were inspired by God to write the Bible, and the extra-scriptural words of men. Her final answer is always, Scripture, yes; agreement on interpretation, no. God, yes; man, no. This suspiciousness of human language, even of her own—the literary analogue to her distrust of everything else merely human—is what accounts for Mrs. Hutchinson's apparent deviousness and inconsistency and for much of what appears to be lying. Piety, not sophistry, pushes her into the corner. If in her view there is "nayther faith, nor knowledge nor Gifts and Graces no nor Life itselfe but all is in Christ Jesus" and "not in us", then everything fades before the inexpressible and everything human is annihilated before the divine. At the same time her anxiety in the face of this dislocation produces an irritating and disjointed hair-splitting when she is talking about the Bible in contrast to a more dense and poetical kind of speech when she is not: *"I thinke the soule to be nothing but Light"*; as well as a sharp wit: "Do you think it not lawful for me to teach women and why do you call me to teach the court?"

The problem is that though the doctrine—the indwelling of the Spirit —implies some kind of entrance by the divine into the human person, the exact sense in which this phenomenon is understood is far from clear. As Winthrop points out, there is a question whether indwelling is by "gifts and power only, or by any other manner of presence, seeing the scripture doth not declare it." If she held, as accused, "that we have no Grace in our Selves but all is in Christ and thear is no inherent Righteousnes in us", Mrs. Hutchinson had to be looking for something more than the entrance of "gifts and power." The difference is between Thomas Hooker saying that in conversion "a kinde of light is let into the soule" and Mrs. Hutchinson seeing the soul itself as "nothing but Light." She wants more than qualities—she wants substance; and in this quest she is after all only taking literally what her teacher, Cotton, repeatedly stresses: that one sign of grace is the conviction that "all your owne parts are empty things in comparison of Christ" and that "such as have Christ in truth, and so having him, have life by him; they do not rest in having any of the benefits of Christ, though they be spirituall, but they cheifely affect to have himselfe, not so much his benefits as himselfe." Unlike Cotton, however, Mrs. Hutchinson cannot be sure that having Christ gives the "power to expresse your selves in company," to "hear or pray aright."

To such a mind it is not evident, as it is to Thomas Dudley with his Ramist reasoning, that "if they do not preach a covenant of grace clearly, then they preach a covenant of works." There is no guarantee of clarity: "No Sir, one may preach a covenant of grace more clearly than another, so I said". For Mrs. Hutchinson it is as if everyone's "parts" or abilities are doomed to perpetual emptiness in comparison of Christ, that even after

union there is no assurance of that "elevation of reason" and that "freshening and quickening of the understanding" which Perry Miller defined as the Puritans' idea of grace and which permits a measure of confidence in enlightened, coherent human discourse. Insofar as Mrs. Hutchinson's extreme piety leads her so inexorably into the ineffable divine that she seems, at least implicitly, to deny the human faculties, she is not a true disciple of Cotton, nor is she the apostle of unity but of separation. It is her adversaries, the Puritan ministers, who try to hold in delicate balance the contact between the supernatural and the natural, insisting that grace is an infusion of qualities from God. Even Cotton, who surpasses the other ministers with his "having Christ we have all" (not just his benefits), would have agreed with Thomas Hooker that the inlet is also an outlet and that the regenerate soul attains to a mutual "intercourse with the Almighty," meeting "as really with him in the Actions of Understanding, as the Eye meets with the Light in Seeing."

If human language is imprecise and uninformed before grace and swept away in a tidal wave of spirit after grace, then words cannot consistently be relied upon to fulfill their basic denotative function, as Susanne Langer defines it, of relating "at once to a conception, which may be ever so vague, and to a *thing* (or event, quality, person, etc.) which is realistic and public." This assumption is borne out in Mrs. Hutchinson's testimony by her tendency to separate words from their referents—and never more so than in treating of the operation of grace itself.

Mr. Cotten. Sister was thear not a Time when once you did hould that thear was *no distinct graces inherent in us but all was in Christ Jesus?*

Mrs. Hutchison. *I did mistake the word In-herent*, as Mr. Damphord [Davenport] can tell who did cause me first to see my Mistake in the word inherent. . . .
Mr. Shephard. She did not only deny the word inherent, but denied the very Thinge itself. Than I asked her if she did beleave that the spirit of God was in Beleevers.
Mrs. Hutchison. *I confes my Expressions was that way but it was never my Judgment.*
Mr. Damphord. It requiers you to answer playnly in thease Thinges.

Sargeon Oliver [questioning a remark that seemed to disparage "Creature Graces"] . . . Now if you doe not deny *created Graces in us* than cleer that Expression.
Mrs. Hutchison. I confesse I have denied the Word Graces but not the Thinge itself.

Similarly, Mrs. Hutchinson divides speaking from being: "I might say [of the ministers] they might preach a covenant of works as did the apostles, but to preach a covenant of works and to be under a covenant of works is another business". This can be construed as simple hedging (Mrs. Hutchinson has rashly accused the ministers of not being "sealed with the spirit" of grace in the first place); it is also a statement about language.

According to David D. Hall:

Mrs. Hutchinson based her attack upon the "legall" preachers on the difference between these covenants [of works and grace]. Between free grace and man's own righteousness she saw no connection, and therefore insisted on treating sanctification as a "work." From the radical disjunction between grace and "duties" flowed the rhetoric of the Antinomians.

But the trial records suggest that Anne Hutchinson treated language itself as one of those "works" or "duties"—an external sign, an action, which could not be regarded as evidence of grace. That is why preaching a covenant is not the same as being under that covenant, why speech is no assurance of one's personal spiritual state. If words are indeed works, we may even substitute *thought* and *word* for *grace* and *righteousness* in Hall's sentence, and consider that between the very thought or opinion or judgment, and the word or expression, Anne Hutchinson saw little or no "connection." That is what made her sound like a liar when she said, "I have denied the Word. . .but not the Thinge itselfe"; and "My Judgment is not altered though my Expression alters." Sanctification is no sure evidence of justification. Words are no sure evidence of conceptions.

• • •

In their endeavor to keep head and heart united, the Puritans were deeply convinced of the reliability of language. Nothing was more fundamental to that conviction than the power of words to beget emotions, to stir the affections. For John Winthrop's father, "the only report" of Mistress Margaret's "modest behauiour, and mielde nature" was sufficient to "breede in my heart" a strong "fatherly Loue and affection" towards his future daughter-in-law. In every conversion relation the heart is quickened by the preacher's elucidation of the Word. But Anne Hutchinson's rejection of the preachers, even of Cotton, is symptomatic of her unorthodox perceptions. She conforms to William James's definition of the religious mind, in which inarticulate feelings of reality precede any rational process. "I do believe," said James, "that feeling is the deeper source of religion, and that philosophic and theological formulas are secondary products, like translations of a text nto another tongue." The attribution of a secondary importance to verbal formulations, the distinction between feeling as one language and creed as another, is what we have been noting in Anne Hutchinson. It may fairly be said that her verbal behavior was what her adversaries most despised about her. She was intolerable to them because she called attention to the failure of language to operate according to their expectations. If it is a law of the mind that form controls matter, as Perry Miller said, then Mrs. Hutchinson's loosening of the form of language, her ambiguities and arbitrariness, must have seemed a threat to the very foundation of things. Mrs. Hutchinson's "lye" was not a trumped-up charge, but a viscerally felt moral wrong.

• • •

Why should this schism have developed? What happened to Anne Hutchinson, and presumably to some if not all of the members of her "potent party", to turn the city on a hill into a tower of Babel?

The Puritans brought with them to New England a special mixture of oral and literate cultures which, as Walter J. Ong has pointed out, particularly characterized the Renaissance and the Reformation. According to Ong, the combination of old oral-aural frames of mind with a new stress on the written, printed word "imposed curious new pressures on the psyche. At the time when the long-impending breakthrough to typography was achieved and the religious crisis of the Reformation took form, the word was present to man in most curious and confusing guises." A major reason for the confusion was that oral culture is essentially tribal—a culture of shared meaning in which the word is "socially unitive." A book, on the other hand, "takes the reader out of the tribe" and throws him on his own inner resources

in a radically new way. The Puritans insisted on the right of individuals to read the Bible privately, but their preoccupation with the "plain" sense of the Scriptures complicated matters by compelling the reader to return—book in hand, so to speak—to the tribe, to a community of saintly readers who somehow could be relied upon to agree on the one true sense of Scripture, and to hold meaning steady through "communal continuation." Unfortunately, "the disconcerting fact that no longer could everyone be so relied on showed that communal structures and psychological structures had changed," and undoubtedly these changes were in turn accelerated by the impact of the new and conflicting modes of literary expression.

Anne Hutchinson exemplifies the problem because she herself is a curious and evidently unsuccessful hybrid of "oral-aural" and "literate" characteristics, in a culture not wholly dominated by either mode. The trial records, containing all that we have of her actual words, indicate that Mrs. Hutchinson was much more adept at hearing sermons and remembering words—both oral skills—than she was at reading and analyzing Scripture. For example, Mrs. Hutchinson, not surprisingly, sounds like John Cotton much of the time. "You know Sir what he doth declare though he doth not know himself" could be a blurred reflection of this passage from *Christ the Fountain*: "It is true, it may be many a good soule cannot readily tell you, what promise did first bring them on to God; but though thou canst not alwayes tell, yet a word of promise it was." Elsewhere Winthrop reports that "she said she walked by the rule of the Apostle, *Gal.* which she called the rule of the new creature, but what rule that was, she would not, or she could not tell." Mrs. Hutchinson may have been remembering the same sermon from *Christ the Fountain*, in which Cotton bases the rule of the "new creature" on Gal 3:5, preaching that "we cannot have a spirit of life wrought in us by the workes of the Law, nor by the words of the Law." For years, Mrs. Hutchinson had been hearing Cotton link works with words in this way, or equate verbal activities with "duties," as he did in his Salem sermon of 1636 (just as the Antinomian Controversy was beginning to boil over): "Now then, doth the Lord draw you to Christ, when you are broken in the sense of your own sins, and of your own righteousness? When you look at duties you are not able to do them, not able to hear or pray aright."

Still another instance of Mrs. Hutchinson's listening powers has to do with Thomas Hooker's *Farewell Sermon*, which she is said to have quoted on the voyage to America. If the report by her acquaintance, Mr. Bartholomew, is correct, she cannot really be faulted for telling him, "He said thus—it was revealed to me yesterday that England should be destroyed." Hooker did exclaim, "Suppose God hath told me this night that he will destroy England, and lay it waste, what say you brethren to it?" and though he offered some hope that disaster might still be averted, the sermon concentrated on England's almost certain doom. Yet the ministers persist in calling her recollection inaccurate and even challenge Cotton to explain "that about the destruction of England"; and in the end Shepard calls it one of her "fayned and fantasticall Revelations". The fact is that Mrs. Hutchinson's memory of the emotional tenor of Hooker's sermon is close to the mark.

On the other hand, although her recall of Bible passages is also impressive, Mrs. Hutchinson's interpretations of them are often faulty. She is wrong about 2 Cor 3:6, "Who also hath made us able ministers of the new testament; not of the letter, but of the spirit." Mrs. Hutchinson disputed this verse with one of the ministers, Nathaniel Ward: "He said that was the letter of the law. No said I it is the letter of the gospel". According to scholars then and now, Ward was right: "the letter" in this verse is the old covenant, or Mosaic law. But Mrs. Hutchinson's reading supports her feeling that the Bay Colony ministers are preaching a covenant of works, and that, as Winthrop reports it, "they had not the seal of the spirit".

She is also highly unorthodox in deriving from Scripture the conviction *"that the Soules of all Men by nature are mortall and die like Beastes"*. This is the notion that so distresses Winthrop by "destroying" everything human. Shocking her opponents by claiming that at the death of the body, unregenerate "souls" die forever while regenerate "spirits" live eternally (and thus, to the ministers' horrified ears, sweeping away with one stroke the future punishment of the wicked), Mrs. Hutchinson is unable to defend what amounts to a semantically heretical position. She compounds the problem by insisting that the Bible tells her so—that her definitions of the word *soul* and the word *spirit* come from the Word of God and that her reading of Scripture convinces her that whatever the human soul is, it is forever linked with the flesh, and entirely distinct from the special and incorporeal spirit that comes from and belongs to God. To prove it, she calls in verses from Ecclesiastes, Luke, 1 Thessalonians and Hebrews—despite all that Cotton can do to reinterpret the evidence ("Sister doe not shut your Eyes agaynst the Truth. All these places prove that the soule is Immortall" and —even more puzzling—despite the exegeses of all these passages readily available in the *Geneva Bible*.

• • •

Cotton (who himself uses the words *soul* and *spirit* more or less interchangeably throughout the trial) finally tries to break through the lexical confusion by reminding his pupil that there is an ever-reliable remedy: she could have kept a clear mind in these matters by properly hearing the Word preached, if not by reading it for herself.

> You have no scripture to prove this. Therefor you ought not to prostitute your Fayth to any one no not to your owne Inventions. And you have herd playne places against it as that the *Spirits of wicked men are in Hell:* and you have herd that the soules of the faythfull are in Heaven.

Cotton has put his finger on the glaring mistake Mrs. Hutchinson makes with the Scriptures: that she bends the Word to support her own presuppositions. This is the kind of thinking we might expect in an oral culture, where all truths are already given and merely reworked and rephrased in cyclical story and song. But in Puritan New England it is simply wrong; it is the spiritualizing of the Bible which so disgusts Winthrop: "Nothing but a word comes to her mind . . . and this is her revelations." The proper procedure, described by the English nonconformist Richard Baxter, was based on the assumption that

> we must not try the Scriptures by our most spiritual apprehensions, but our apprehensions by the Scriptures: that is, we must prefer the Spirit's inspiring the apostles to indite the Scriptures, before the Spirit's illuminating of us to understand them, or before any present inspirations, the former being the more perfect.

The type of mind William James described, which puts feelings before all rational process, would indeed "try the Scriptures by its most spiritual apprehensions," and that is what Mrs. Hutchinson does. Yet her outburst of "revelations" in the General Court suggests that she is also puzzled by Scripture and that she wants confidence in the exercise of her own faculties: "Who then was antichrist? Was the Turk antichrist only? The Lord knows that I could not open scripture; he must by his prophetical office open it unto me." But the worst of it is that she carries on a perilous flirtation with typology.

> Then this place in Daniel was brought unto me and did shew me that though I should meet with affliction yet I am the same God that delivered Daniel out of the lion's den, I will also deliver thee. —Therefore I desire you to look to it, for you see this scripture fulfilled this day.

Mrs. Hutchinson here drops right into the trap Perry Miller described as "the danger . . . that typologists might torture the Old Testament to yield up private fancies." And this is, to the Puritans, a linguistic crime.

Mrs. Hutchinson's patterns of hearing and reading, then, are erratic: sometimes clear, sometimes foggy, like her speech. In neither case is there any real assurance of a body of accepted common meanings by which she can test her perceptions. Despite all the talk about Puritan "plain-sense" and despite Reform Protestantism's insistence on the fact that there is "but" one sense belongs to one Scripture . . . there is but one literal meaning," there was no absolute agreement on what "the Grammar of it"—the basic, rock-bottom sense of it—really was; and yet the society insisted that everyone adhere to the single truth of things. That communal continuation to which Ong refers, which is the only framework for such unanimity, had suffered too many strains. There was still a remnant of it—a remnant which allowed the Court sincerely to proclaim, "We know the mind of the party without . . . testimony" or "Ey, but she intended this that they say". But there was not enough of it to keep Mrs. Hutchinson from protesting, "My name is precious and you do affirm a thing which I utterly deny".

One more element in the Puritan "culture mix" which undoubtedly had a deep effect on Mr. Hutchinson and on her allies was the problem not of expression, but of non-expression. The Puritans never claimed that everything could be explained. Perry Miller wrote that when the question of God's immanence in the universe became too difficult, "preachers often avoided the issue, declaring, 'this is but a curious question: therefore I will leave it,' or remarking that the Lord fills both heaven and earth, . . . 'but in an incomprehensible manner, which we cannot expresse to you.'" Yet, of all the knotty Puritan questions, none was more inexpressible or unexpressed than that of the union of the soul with Christ. None was treated less often and less explicitly than the actual moment of conversion, even though it was one of the cardinal subjects in the Antinomian Controversy and in Puritan life.

At the same time, it was demanded of ordinary people that they find a way to describe this indescribable mystery, since, in order to gain membership in most New England churches, one was required to give a spoken relation of one's conversion experience. In effect, the demonstration of sainthood called for language which most of the ministers themselves were unable or unwilling to exemplify. Spiritual autobiographies might provide general models, and detailed prescriptions were dictated by ministers like Shepard in his sermon series, *The Parable of the Ten Virgins*, but prescriptions are precisely the problem: they squeeze the individual, the empirical, the spontaneous into a Procrustean bed of formulaic language and weaken the vital connections between outer words and inner meaning. John S. Coolidge claims that there is no evidence that anyone was ever refused church membership on the grounds that his relation was unconvincing, and that the "only aspect of them which could be called a 'test' was doctrinal." This may have been reassuring for those who could memorize catechisms, but it would not have been salutary for the life and enrichment of the language. And in fact by the end of the century the conversion relation was becoming nothing more than "'a quaint Speech in the Church.'"

Where, then, could people like Anne Hutchinson turn for a language to accord with their most vital and deeply felt experiences? There were some vivid accounts of the conversion experience emanating from the continental Reform movement and from the more radical segment of English Puritanism represented by the preacher Thomas Goodwin, who experienced a "direct communication from God himself"—very much like Anne Hutchinson! God, we are told, "took him aside and said to him privately, 'Do you now turn to me, and I will pardon all your sins tho never so many, as I forgave and pardoned my Servant Paul.'" One wonders how different this account is from Mrs. Hutchinson's Daniel story. Goodwin's sermons were published in 1636, the year of the beginning of the Antinomian Controversy, out whether Mrs. Hutchinson read (or had heard) them, or others like them, is not known.

On this side of the ocean, however, the lack of explicitness and consistency on a question of the most urgent nature, within a religious community which laid a major claim to clarity of language, undoubtedly fostered verbal confusion. Robert Middlekauf, in his study of Puritan piety and intellect, has shown that for the Puritans, codes and ideas pre-shaped and controlled emotions, transmuting "raw feeling" into feeling sanctioned by society. Yet on this seminal issue there was no clear-cut and comforting code to tell people how they were expected to feel. Given a personality like Anne Hutchinson's in such a situation, the wild "revelations" of her court trial are no surprise. In the face of a serious language vacuum, the only alternative was the burst of more or less formulaic conversion relations which became widespread at just about this time in New England.

Yvor Winters has pointed out that the ejection of Anne Hutchinson launched a new kind of society in which "objective evidence . . . took the place of inner assurance, and the behavior of the individual took on symbolic value." On the linguistic front, the conversion relation appears to be a herald of this trend. It is important for two reasons. The conversion relation shies away from the as-yet-inexpressible, and in doing so it abandons a vast portion of human experience at the frontiers of verbal accessibility. Consequently, with its intrenchment, the public and private, the outer and inner modes of language are wrenched a little further apart. These are the very problems, stated in a different way, with which our examination of the Antinomian Controversy began; problems of separation which in one form or another have persisted in American life and literature, and which point up the urgent necessity to recover, especially in and through language, what Winters calls "the permeation of human experience by a consistent moral understanding."

When John Cotton presented his long admonition at Mrs. Hutchinson's church trial, he was making one last attempt to come down firmly on the side of the tribe and on the side of language. He recognized that Mrs. Hutchinson's difficulties, despite her sociability and her standing in the community, were the rumblings of a fateful rupture in "communal continuation," evidenced not only by the fact that "God hath left you to your selfe" and not only by *"the greate hurt you have done to the Churches"* but also by the horrifying possibility that, if her views should prevail, "what need we care what we speake, or doe?".

Mrs. Hutchinson herself seems to have felt the danger. When she interrupted Cotton's speech to say that *"I did not hould any of thease Thinges before my Imprisonment"*, her lie bespoke some faint last-minute realization that not only language but thought itself is a social phenomenon, and that in isolation one finally can lose hold of the sense of truth.

In any case, the language problems raised in the Antinomian Controversy were not resolved. And Mrs. Hutchinson spent the long last portion of her church trial in utter silence.

The Sexual Dimension

The attitude of the Massachusetts judges toward Anne Hutchinson was influenced by her sex. As Englishmen of the seventeenth century John Winthrop and his fellow magistrates believed that the role appropriate for women was a domestic one. Even an orthodox woman such as the talented poetess Anne Bradstreet was made to feel the disapproval of society for her intellectual pursuits; and Anne Bradstreet was the daughter of one governor of the colony and the wife of another. Yet if the traditional values of Englishmen placed restraints on female endeavors, the spirit of Protestantism promised women a new importance. Ben Barker-Benfield examines these forces and offers his views on how they contributed to the Antinomian controversy.

BEN BARKER-BENFIELD

"Anne Hutchinson and the Puritan Attitude Toward Women"

Historians of the Antinomian Controversy, 1636-1638, from Charles Francis Adams in 1892, to J.K. Hosmer in 1908, and most recently, David Hall in 1968 have generally agreed with John Winthrop in his assessment of the danger it posed to the existence of New England. The controversy between Winthrop's New England Way and the Hutchinsonians (the Antinomians) was "the sorest tryall that ever befell us since we left our Native soyle." If Winthrop's faction had not been helped by God, the old Serpent, Satan, "would soon have driven Christ and Gospel out of New England . . . and [have led] to the repossessing of Satan in his ancient Kingdom." Satan's "instrument . . . so fitted and trained to his service for interrupting the passage [of the] Kingdome in this part of the world," was, as it was at the time of his first temptation of man, a woman.

In some respects Anne Hutchinson represented the emergence of dynamic individaul consciousness as a potential for everyone after the Reformation. "Mrs. Hutchinson, like Hampden, Lilburne, Winstanley, and many more, heralded the arrival of that new man who was to be so startlingly delineated by Rousseau a century later; an uncommon man who struggled to break down the restrictive barriers of an organic society, who demanded full freedom to assert his talents and idiosyncrasies." At the same time, it seems odd, given Hutchinson's sex and the nature of her dispute with the godly males of Massachusetts Bay, that she should have heralded a new man. The oddity is not simply the result of the confusion between the two meanings of "man," that is species generic (the sense in which it is used in the preceding quotation), and sex-specific. The revolution in which Hampden, Lilburne, Winstanley—and Winthrop— were engaged on behalf of the new man (species generic) also erected or renewed a barrier on behalf of the new man (sex-specific), and against the emergence of the new woman. Winthrop's struggle with Hutchinson bears out Levin Schückling's suggestion (endorsed by Ian Watt) that Reformation individualism devalued women and accelerated the separation of the sexes.

This article's hypothesis is that men effectively excluded women from the "priesthood of all believers," the idea that everyone was brought to "a direct experience of the spirit and removed intermediaries between himself and the deity . . . that [all] regenerate men [species generic] were illumined with divine truth" and therefore were priests unto themselves; that women might feel themselves excluded from the relief afforded men by covenant theology (defined below); that Anne Hutchinson's antinomianism was in part, at least, a response to the need thereby created in women; that Winthrop recognized that response; and that his own reaction was largely influenced by what he perceived as a sexual threat; that this sexual threat was intensified by Hutchinson's role as midwife; that the explanation for the Puritan invidiousness in the treatment of women, and the virulence of Winthrop's response to Hutchinson lay in the male need to give more definition to men and to God than the initial Protestant dynamic had allowed, and to find an objective correlative for such definition in the sexual relationship.

• • •

Seventeenth-century Puritan rebels in England had denied the authority of priest, bishop, and king to mediate between the individual and God. They had asserted the priesthood of all believers. But once they had won power and had become part of what the historian G.H. Williams calls the "magisterial" and "classical" Reformation in Europe, these men constituted themselves a mediating caste, especially in the eyes of those groups Williams describes as constituting the "radical Reformation." The New England Puritans and their Hutchinsonian opponents had already extended the magisterial/radical conflict to the New World, and Winthrop was perfectly accurate in associating the Hutchinsonians with Familists, Libertines, and the Anabaptists of Münster—groups whose names were watchwords for religious and sexual anarchy in the seventeenth century.

Both Williams and Keith Thomas have pointed out the meaning for women of the Protestant tenet of the priesthood of all believers. Williams describes how it worked doctrinally— "the extension of the priesthood of the Christophorous laity to women"— and Thomas relates the premise to the prominence of women both in positions of leadership and in sheer numbers in the Civil War Sects" in old England, that is almost contemporaneously with the rise of the

Hutchinsonians in New England. In traditional patriarchal society (already undercut by the individualizing tendencies of magisterial Protestantism) speaking women were, by definition, rebels. Female sectarians reproduced in the family the religious divisiveness Puritans created for the established churches, challenging men to make good for women what they claimed for themselves.

• • •

The "dictatorship" or "oligarchy" ruling the churches of Massachusetts Bay, comprising a heirarchy of ministers, elders, teachers and deacons, were all male, chosen by men; it controlled the terms of acceptance into church membership—as much social and formal recognition of visible salvation as an individual could get. Existentially, such recognition placed the member much closer to God. At "a time in which the beyond meant everything, when the social position of the Christian depended on his admission to the communion, the clergyman, through his ministry, Church discipline, and preaching, exercised an influence . . . which we modern men are entirely unable to picture." Moreover, it was only the male members of the church who could vote for the political magistracy —the General Court. The magistrates at both of Hutchinson's trials, political and religious, were all men. Men ran the society which expressed the covenant with God. And all men were, by definition, closer to God than women. Man was the "conveyance" between God and creation, including woman. Her mind was weaker, or conversely, her more earthly ties were stronger. As husbands and fathers, all men represented the magistracy in their households.

• • •

The patterns of authority in New England were intended to facilitate the expressions of the will of God, both inwardly in the matter of individual salvation, and outwardly by the control of all the forms of civil life. It may be that any human expression of the will of God was impossible, since it amounted to the sacreligious unveiling of Calvin's awesome vision of God, that is, pure will. God's most significant act for humanity was his predestination of a few to heaven and his damnation of the rest to hell. Since God was pure will, he was unpredictable and unknowable; so people had to abide in ignorance of their most crucial fate. In the late sixteenth and early seventeenth centuries, some of Calvin's heirs in England—the intellectual authorities of the Puritan settlers in America—elaborated the attempts to live with such a God into a variant theological system which Perry Miller has described exhaustively. He labeled it "covenant theology."

• • •

The idea of God's totality of power had to be reconciled with men's knowing, and therefore sharing enough of it to be able to recognize the evidence that would supply them with some existential reassurance of salvation and allow them to judge themselves worthy of church membership. The "human intellect" best fitted to struggle in the coils of covenant theology was the one closest to God, that is, it was male. Control of admission to church membership was monopolized on the basis of sex. Women could well have perceived such a social reality as an obstacle to salvation: How were women to deal with this tangible representation of the belief that they were intrinsically incapable of the theological expertise available to the more godlike intellect of a man? If covenant theology was constructed to soften the unmitigated tension of living under God's unknowable omnipotence (its most crucial expression—the salvation or domnation of the individual soul), and if males exclusively handled the softening operation, then perhaps women still had to live more closely to the unsoftened glare of God's unknowableness.

•••

Hutchinson invalidated the divines' contract with God, which, in effect, had sanctioned and rewarded their own efforts toward salvation, and, conversely, made it more difficult for women to relate directly to God. She argued that "Christ was all, did all, and that the soule remained as a dead Organ." She rescued total "dependance" on God from Puritan ambivalence toward the idea, and made it all-sufficient. Winthrop described how "the maine and bottom of all [of the Hutchinsonians' beliefs], which tended to quench all indevor, and to bring to a dependance upon an immediate witnesse of the Spirit, without sight of any gift or grace, this stuck fast . . . to have nothing, but waite for Christ to do all . . . And indeed most of her new tenents tended towards slothfulnesse, and quench all indevor in the creature." It should be repeated at this point that Winthrop and his fellow magistrates held themselves wholly dependent on the will of God, even as their commitment to the sanctification process of covenant theology undid such total dependence completely, and, in effect, helped make men gods to themselves and to their families.

The Hutchinsonians forced Winthrop's nose into the fundamental contradiction between enacting God's (unknowable) will, and being totally passive in the light of God's omnipotence. Furthermore, it was a woman, that creature whose essential nature he supposed to be as passively dependent on him as his was on God, who

had raised the issue. And furthermore, the Puritans' own most persistent metaphor for the passive, dependent side of their relation to God was a sexual one, more appropriate, one might think, to those dependent on the gods men were to them.

Edmund Morgan has described the way in which New England Puritans construed their union to Christ in sexual terms. The elect man was a "bride" to Christ, the "bridegroom." Their union was "marriage" which was consummated to produce the "fruit" of a "new birth." As friends of the groom, ministers served to arrange the match, according to the marriage custom of the time. Morgan quotes these words of John Cotton. "The publick Worship of God is the bed of loves: where, 1. Christ embraceth the souls of his people, and casteth into their hearts the immortal seed of his Word, and Spirit, Gal. 4.19. 2. The Church conceiveth and bringeth forth fruits to Christ." Morgan suggests that this sexual metaphor was the dominant one in the characterization of the union between man and God. So Hutchinson's challenge to the set forms of the contract between man and God, and her demand that it be replaced by simple "justification" unmediated by God's male friends, and Winthrop's response to challenge and demand, were couched in such a sexual idiom.

On the face of it, there does not seem to be much difference between Hutchinson's calling Christ's "the voyce of my beloved," and Winthrop's ecstatic account of his relationship with Christ: "methought my soule has as familiar and sensible society with him as wife could have with the kindest husbande; I desired no other happinesse but to be embraced of him; I held nothinge so deere that I was not willinge to parte with for him; I forgatt to looke after my supper, and some vaine things that my heart lingered after before; then came such a calme of comforte over my heart, as revived my spirits, set my minde and conscience at sweet liberty and peace." Winthrop here represented himself as a woman being embraced by Christ, whose apparent sexual identity was male. Winthrop's use of such a mode required him to change his view of himself (from male to female)—something Hutchinson did not have to do. Women could slip into Christ's arms without any preliminary step—that is, had not the male caste intervened in the relationship. All creatures, including women "had access to God only through their superior, man."

Hutchinson and her associates asked that the priesthood of all believers be body-blind. That was a central purpose of her concentration on the nature of "union" with Christ. One result of "justification," of conversion, was the shedding of the body, and of sexual delimitations: "the soul is mortal, till it be united to Christ, and then it is annihilated, and the body also, and a new given by Christ." As if to underscore this assertion of the insignificance of the earthly body, another of Hutchinson's "errors" was the belief that "there is no resurrection of the body." According to the radical Reformation, which the Hutchinsonians represented, believers became demi-gods, beyond the sexual distinction. And Hutchinson's brother-in-law, John Wheelwright, modified the sexual analogy in light of that transfiguration. Union with God "of necessity...must be personal, and so a believer must be more than a creature, viz., God-man, even Christ Jesus. For though in a true union the two terms may still remain the same, etc., as between a husband and wife, he is a man still, and she a woman, (for the union is only in

sympathy and relation), yet in a real or personal union [i.e., with God] it is not." The Hutchinsonians held that union with God, the superordinate goal of their society, transcended sex.

It is in such a context of body-blindness that one should read Hutchinson's warning to the men judging her, obsessed as they were by Anne's repudiation of the role their values said her body dictated: "take heed what yee goe about to doe unto me, for you have no power over my body, neither can you do me any harme, for I am in the hands of the eternall Jehovah my Saviour." Hutchinson took the terms of salvation beyond those controlled by men. Her opening a "faire and easie way to Heaven," a point Winthrop swelt on with scorn, had a special meaning for women.

Theologically speaking, the "calling" to which Winthrop assigned Hutchinson and all women, that of housewife, might be regarded as just as advantageous a position for election as any that men could follow. But the issue should be considered from the women's own point of view, that is, existentially. As we have seen, she was excluded from the formulation and control of her society's major ends; in the most general and tangible senses, she was inferior to man in her relation to God. Indeed, she was taught to look on him as the representative of the God she was obliged to worship and obey. Besides, the signs of a successful fulfillment of the housewifely calling were much harder to come by than those of the callings available to man. Men could familiarize themselves with the knotty niceties of covenant theology (and thereby blunt the uncertainty) or at least identify with those who could.

• • •

At the time of Anne Hutchinson's rise (and interspersed in Winthrop's account of it) there were several cases of women driven to desperation by the horrors of uncertainty which covenant theology was supposed, in some sense, to alleviate. In 1637 a "woman of Boston congregation, having been in much trouble of mind about her spiritual estate, at length grew into utter desperation, and could not endure to hear of any comfort, etc., so as one day she took her little infant and threw it into a well, and then came into the house and said, now she was sure she should be damned, for she had drowned her child; but some stepping presently forth, saved the child." Puritans lived their lives as potentially God's children but on the brink of the Devil's well, and in this case, a woman managed to play God to herself.

The sexual arbitrariness of husband and his echoing magistracy vs. the "spiritual delusions" of a woman's mind shaped another case, in 1638, some of whose features combined those of Hutchinson's insubordination with those of the woman dropping herself into hell. Dorothy Talbye had been a good church member, but "falling at difference with her husband, through melancholy or spiritual delusions," she tried at different times to kill him, herself and her children, "saying it was so revealed," i.e., by God's voice, as Hutchinson had finally condemned herself by claiming God spoke directly to her. The magistrates cast her out, after "much patience and divers admonitions." Their action made her "worse," and the magistrates responded by having her whipped. Her "reform" consisted in her carrying herself "more dutifully to her husband." But then, like Hutchinson, she showed herself "possessed with Satan [who] persuaded her by his delusions, which she listened to as revelations from God" to take that course taken by the

woman who had cast her child into a well, and for the same reason, "to break the neck of her own child, that she might be free from future misery."

The magistrates did to Dorothy Talbye what she had done to her child —they hanged her. She remained committed to her own fuller selfhood to the end, desiring to be beheaded, since "it was less painful and less shameful." Winthrop and the magistrates (including Hugh Peter) seem to have associated Dorothy Talbye with Hutchinson (as Talby's own, proud bearing seems to have done, too). Hutchinson's and Talbye's stories are interleaved in Winthrop's *Journal*: at her execution, "Mr. Peter gave an exhortation to the people to take heed of revelations, etc., and of despising the ordinance of excommunication as she [and Hutchinson] had done; for when it was to have been denounced against her, she turned her back, and would have gone forth, if she had not been stayed by force."

There was a third case of a woman challenging the godly magistracy in 1638, a Mistress Oliver, like Dorothy Talbye from Salem, for "ability of speech, and appearance of zeal and devotion far before Mrs. Hutchinson." Like Hutchinson and her followers, she defied the "classical" form of sanctification, citing the gospel as her authority for election and membership of the church. She bypassed the magistrates' mediation of her marriage with Christ; "she openly called for it, and stood to plead her right, though she were denied." She "would not forbear, before the magistrate, Mr. Endecott, did threaten to send the constable to put her forth." Her views were Hutchinsonian, and she persisted in them. "After about five years, this woman was adjudged to be whipped for reproaching the magistrates." Winthrop's standard for judging the psychology of such insubordinate women was a sexual one: if Hutchinson and Mistress Oliver were not conventional housewives, then they were manlike. Hutchinson was "of haughty and fierce carriage, of a nimble wit and active spirit, and a very voluble tongue, more bold than a man." Mistress Oliver stood at her whipping "without tying, and bore her punishment with a masculine spirit." Women were not to speak in ways uncontrolled by men. "She had a cleft stick put in her tongue half an hour, for reproaching the elders." These cases make it plain that some women were under considerable pressure in Massachusetts, and responded to it in precisely the terms to which Hutchinson addressed herself.

Winthrop's response to Hutchinson demonstrates the extent to which he felt her a sexual threat. It is hard to imagine Winthrop venting the extreme language quoted in the first paragraph of this article had the sexual dimension not been present. Hutchinson set the Puritan world topsy-turvy. Her classes of sixty, even eighty, at a time were composed predominantly of women, and were, in Winthrop's view, the occasions for the mass reversal of sexual subordination—all of these women were leaving their place. It was resolved that "though women might meet (some few together) to pray and edify one another; yet such a set assembly (as was then in practice at Boston) where sixty or more did meet every week, and one woman (in a prophetical way, by resolving questions of doctrine, and expanding scripture) took upon her the whole exercise, was agreed to be disorderly, and without rule." The meetings were condemned for being "publick" and "frequent," and what was taught there was not "that which the Apostle commands [women] viz., to keep at home." Hutchinson's exer-

cise of instruction "drawes them, and by occasion thereof many families are neglected, and much time lost, and a great damage comes to the Common-wealth thereby, which wee that are betrusted with, as the Fathers of the Common-wealth, are not to suffer." The magistrates saw Hutchinson's disruption of the individual family patriarchate projected on to a general scale. They held that she should not teach at all—because she was a woman. Hutchinson pointed out their inconsistency here: they had allowed that older women could teach younger women.

Time and again Winthrop alluded to the "division between husband and wife" caused by Hutchinson's teachings. On one occasion he seemed suddenly to bethink himself how the exchange between the court of godly males and the extraordinarily well-versed female theologian was only further expanding such mutinous terms. "We do not mean to discourse with those of your sex but only this; you do adhere to them, and do endeavour to set forward this faction and so you do dishonor us." The men wanted to make Hutchinson subject to their authority, not to engage that part of her that was bolder than a man.

Hutchinson's disturbing sexual identity was thrown into even sharper relief, not because she was, perhaps, going through the menopause, but because she was a midwife. It was through this virtually exclusively female province—obstetric care—that Hutchinson reached out to address the need which the size and composition of her classes demonstrated was there, and intensely enough to drive some women to murder their children. Women's turning to a midwife, an assistant at the springing forth of life, starkly contrasts with their dumb stifling of self and child where the spiritual assistants were exclusively male.

According to Winthrop, Hutchinson "cunningly dissembled and coloured her opinions . . . and was admitted into the Church, then shee began to go to work, and being a woman very helpful in the times of childbirth, and other occasions of bodily infirmities, and well furnished with means for these purposes, shee easily insinuated herselfe into the affections of many." They were troubled in the way that drove one woman to the well. Winthrop went on to describe Hutchinson's teachings, and approved of them insofar as they were consistent with the "publick Ministry"—of godly men. It was when she began "to set forth her own stuffe," departing from the recommendation of a course of action whose most promising terms (learning, sacred employments) were restricted *de facto* to a special male "priesthood," and substituting for it that "faire and easie way" accessible to everyone equally, that Winthrop accused Hutchinson of "grosse errour," Satanism.

Given the sex of this female "instrument of Satan," her doubly reproductive powers, and the make-up of her classes, it was appropriate that this newly covenanted Christian community, this garden of Christ, should see the theologically curious, rebellious Hutchinson generating a host of Eves, each of them snaring their husbands in the way that Adam had been made to fall, the act the one on which the historical premise of the covenant depended. Hutchinson was the fountainhead of the Antinomians; they "commonly labored to work first upon women, being (as they conceived) the weaker to resist; the more flexible, tender, and ready to yield; and if once they could winde in them, they hoped by them, as by an Eve, to catch their husbands also, which indeed proved too true amongst us." And again, Hutchinson's sex gave a special meaning to a conventional seventeenth-century image, the "seduction" of men's minds. Her followers' use of their sexual powers was a persistent point of reference for Winthrop. He compared them to the "Harlots" who had dealings with a young man (Proverbs, 7:21), even though the Biblical story includes only one harlot, and glossing it in a way that suggests how impossible Winthrop found it to distinguish women's using their tongues independently in speech, from the perverse use of what woman's mouth was expected to do—to kiss: "with much faire speech they caused them to yeeld, with the flattering of their lips they forced them." The metaphor is one of woman raping men. In the final analysis, Hutchinson was the "american Jesabel," and Winthrop specified the Jezebel "mentioned in Revelation" (although that name in both Winthrop and the Bible conjured up Ahab's wife, who "cut off all the prophets of the Lord," I Kings 18:4, and played the harlot, II Kings 9:30). The Jezebel in Revelation used her sexual power to seduce men, body and soul, before the orthodox male God espoused by John of Patmos took charge of Jezebel's sexual power and used it to his own ends. "I have a few things against thee, because thou sufferest that woman, Jezebel, who calleth herself a prophetess, to teach and to seduce my servants to commit fornication, and to eat things sacrificed unto idols. And I gave her space to repent of her fornication, and she repented not. Behold, I will cast her into a bed, and them that commit adultery with her into great tribulation, except they repent of their deeds. And I will kill her children with death; and all the churches shall know that I am he who searcheth the reins and hearts; and I will give unto every one of you according to your works."

So Hutchinson and her female followers were a host of new Eves, threatening the social and theological order imposed by the new Adams. No wonder Winthrop felt that Satan threatened New England with total ruin; his vision of Christ and Gospel being "driven out" suggests, perhaps, the idea of the flight of the earlier bridal pair, Adam and Eve. The vision had an objective correlative in the very topography of settlement.

In view of Hutchinson's Eve-like threat, one can understand how another of her adherents, another midwife, could be labeled a witch. She was Mistress Hawkins, whom Hutchinson had assisted at the birth of Mary Dyer's monster. Mistress Hawkins was "notorious for familiarity with the devill, and now a prime Familist." This "midwife . . . went out of the jurisdiction; and indeed it was time for her to be gone, for it was known, that she used to give young women oil of mandrakes, and other stuff to cause conception; and she grew into great suspicion to be a witch, for it was credibly reported, that when she gave any medicines, (for she practiced physic), she would ask the party, if she did believe, she could help her, etc." Oil of mandrake's root was believed to facilitate conception by arousing man's sexual passion; midwives traditionally played the part Jezebel, Eve, and Anne Hutchinson were held to have played in "seducing" men.

Even in this area—the administration of aphrodisiacs—the behavior of Mistress Hawkins was only a variant of a normal activity in orthodox Puritan society, carried on not only by midwives, but by regular housewives, who grew herbs and simples in their gardens from which they concocted all sorts of medicines for their families. Among them were artichokes, chervil, dill, spearmint and aspargus, all of which were believed to stir up "bodily lust;" women gathered nettles for the same purpose. Christian women were assigned functions that maintained the sense of their closeness to Eve. One can understand Winthrop's concern over Hutchinson's spreading her "poyson" to other housewives, who might then be tempted to take away from their husbands their mastery of their own sexual passions, or failing that, feel justified in killing them.

Winthrop's reference to Mistress Hawkins' Familism (echoing perhaps the phrase "familiarity with the devill") shows how easily female adherents of the radical Reformation (of which the "Family of Love" was part) were associated with promiscuity and witchcraft. The Familists, with whom Winthrop also connected all of the Hutchinsonians by the title of his "Short Story of the Rise, reign, and ruine of the Antinomians, Familists and Libertines" and by his allusions to Hutchinson's doctrines and followers as "Familistical," were like the Libertines (whose name has entered the language) conventionally charged with "moral laxity." Moreover the midwifery role of Anne Hutchinson and Mistress Hawkins only deepened suspicions of their familiarity with the devil's power to use sexuality as Winthrop's account of Mistress Hawkins' attempt to induce fertility might suggest.

For the vast majority of people of the age, midwives were the only doctors. Hutchinson's use of her medical expertise gives a particular historical meaning to the extraordinary persistence of disease and treatment imagery in Winthrop's account of her case, the whole of which he called a "sore." Just like Revelation's Jezebel, Winthrop's

"American Jesabel" gave her patients things to consume. His most frequent characterization of her teaching was "poyson." The "last and worst of all which most suddainly diffused the venome of these opinions into the very veines and vitalls of the People in the Country, was Mistris Hutchinson's doubly weekly-lecture." The midwife-physician dispensed an addictive substance that turned out to be the reverse of therapeutic. "Multitudes of men and women. . .having tasted of [the Hutchinsonians'] Commodities were eager after them, and were streight infected before they were aware, and some being tainted conveyed the infection to others; and thus that Plague first began amongst us." Since midwife-Hutchinson had reversed her therapeutic role, godly men had to assume it. They preached "against those errors, and practices that so much pestered the Countrey, to informe, to confute, to rebuke, etc., thereby to cure those that were diseased already, and to give Antidotes to the rest, to preserve them from infection." Those who refused to relinquish Hutchinsonianism were labeled "incurable" and purged from the social body.

But the physiological metaphor was extended further. It was conventional in ideological disputes in the sixteenth and seventeenth centuries to describe the generation and proliferation of opinions in effusively procreative terms. When the Hutchinsonians continued their teachings in Rhode Island, Winthrop said they were "hatching and multiplying new Opinions." The imagery was consistent with the notion of the fruitful union between Christ and the believer, leading to the rebirth of the latter's soul. Where independent-minded *women* were concerned, the perverse bearing of false opinions seemed to take on a partic-

ularly literal, even gross, quality for Winthrop, who had already found it appropriate to see the intellectual and sexual seductiveness of unorthodox women coincide. Hutchinson had the power to "breed and nourish" factitious beliefs, and to seduce others to them; she bore her own children, and she also assisted other women in parturition. Winthrop saw an intimate connection between Hutchinson's claim to invade male mysteries and her roles in childbearing. The goal of Hutchinson's teachings was the destruction of the control the ministers held over the union with Christ the bridegroom. She wanted to reverse assumptions about women in a way that touched men's theological sexual identities, and this reversal was the more intensely provocative to men because of her prior occupation of perhaps the only powerful social role permitted women—midwifery. Its function made her a superwoman, putting her in charge of mysteries associated with sexuality and fertility. Such power was already close to being Satan's, perhaps because, by definition, it was denied men, but above all because it was Eve's.

When Winthrop crushed Hutchinson, he claimed to assume her midwifery role toward the offspring of her brain, laying them out in the account he published of the whole affair. "The opinions (some of them) were such as these: I say, some of them, to give but a taste, for afterwards you shall see a litter of fourescore and eleven of their brats hung up against the Sunne, besides many new ones of Mistris Hutchinsons, all which they hatched and dandled." And he did the same in broadcasting news of her and her follower Mary Dyer's putative monstrous births, which made tangible their earlier breeding of monstrous opinions—and suggests to what extent such opinions were bound up in Winthrop's imagination with the physiology of their bearers. "God himselfe was pleased to step in with his casting voice, and bring in his owne vote and suffrage from heaven, by testifying his displeasure against their opinions and practices, as clearely as if he had pointed with his finger, in causing the two fomenting women in the time of the height of the Opinions to produce out of their wombs, as before they had out of their braines, such monstrous births as no Chronicle (I thinke) hardly ever recorded the like. Mistris Dier brought forth her birth of a woman child, a fish, a beast, and a fowle, all woven together in one, without a head. . . .

"Mistris Hutchinson being big with child, and growing towards the time of her labor, as other woman doe, she brought forth not one (as Mistris Dier did) but (which was more strange to amazement) 30 monstrous births or thereabouts, at once . . . none at all of them (as farre as I could ever learne) of humane shape." Hutchinson was not only remote from normal women's childbearing, but even from the single monstrosity of Mary Dyer's parturition. Hutchinson's bearing thirty inhuman monsters was appropriate to her creation of all of those Eves at her classes of sixty or more. The godly then "made use of" the monstrous births "in publick," as God used Jezebel's sexual powers in furthering his powers, using them to demonstrate the authority's righteousness. Winthrop's refusal to see Hutchinson's mind apart from her physiology illustrates how accurate Hutchinson was in putting her finger on the profound sexual bias of the operation of grace.

The context for the explanation of Winthrop's attitude to Hutchinson, of the remarkable refusal of Puritans to make good on the priesthood of all

believers as far as women were concerned, and, perhaps, of the asseveration of a sexual relation between men and God, was the fluidity of an identity rooted in contradictions. Puritans destroyed the traditional restraints between man and God and created a more dynamic sense of who man was, and therefore of what he could be. But such adventurousness evoked the appropriate fears of anarchy, of not knowing who they were at all. In other words, the radical psychological, theological and social changes accomplished by Puritan men did not leave them secure enough to permit women the same changes in practice, even though they were conceded to women in theory. On the contrary, these radical changes generated a practical need for men to insist on denying them to women. But the theoretical concession (the idea of the priesthood of all believers, on which the men's own changes was based) generated a continuous process of religious radicalism, whose prophets compounded Puritan anxieties simply by applying Puritan standards more rigorously. That is, they held up to the Puritans precisely the anti-authoritarianism of which the Puritans were guilty. The dissenters could be seen as better Puritans.

• • •

The subordination of women could make men feel they were like God when their other premises might deny it. In the passage in which Winthrop described his love for Christ, and Christ's for him, Christ was to Winthrop as Winthrop was to his wife. The terms make it clear how, existentially, a man could identify with God, and how, consistent with such identification, he needed a given distinction from his wife to affirm such godlikeness. If this sexual distinction had been made irrelevant to the relationship with God (as Hutchinson and her followers argued) then men could have thought of women as much closer to passive "bridehood" to Christ than men were. This line of thought also suggests that, at some level, men wanted to believe that the first discernible quality of an unknowable God was that he, like them, was male.

John Cotton—more learned than Winthrop—was tempted to go Hutchinson's way, but eventually he, too, associated her with the Libertines and the other radical Reformation groups holding most literally to the priesthood of all believers. "You cannot evade the Argument: that filthie Sinne of the Communitie of Woemen; and all promiscuous and filthie comings togeather of men and Woemen without Distinction or Relation of Marriage, will necessarily follow [Hutchinson's teaching] Though I have not herd, nayther do I thinke you have bine unfaythfull to your Husband in his Marriage Covenant yet that will follow upon it." Cotton's prediction focused directly on the Hutchinsonians' claim to God's body blindness, and translated it immediately into the fantasy of sexual order in the relationship on earth that corresponded to God-as-male's relationship to believer-as-female. Again, the terms suggest a man's need to identify with God in his relationship with his wife. I have pointed out how that kind of intervention may have reflected the fear that woman was intrinsically closer to God because of the nature of the sexual metaphor men used to describe the passive, dependent, side of their relationship to God.

Winthrop devalued dependence explicitly in dealing with "mistris Hutchinson," and also in his and his party's adherence to covenant activism, which Hutchinson called "works." Yet the godly magistrates held themselves to be dependent, feminine, toward Christ. In that relationship (which they freed themselves from women to pursue), men felt themselves to show qualities they held degrading. Perhaps they could sustain their espousal of passive, feminine qualities only by reminding themselves of how active, masculine and Christ-like they really were by way of their relationship to those beings they construed as unmitigatedly dependent, that is, to women. But presumably they were dependent on women for their own model of feminine behavior as they received Christ's seed. But again, men's holding women to total dependence on god-men left women more exposed to the pure willfulness of God, or, conversely, women's relationship to God was undiluted by the selfserving legalisms of covenant theology.

This assertion of godlike, manly and independent willfulness by way of dependence on womanly passivity was compressed into a perverse but not unfamiliar metaphor during Hutchinson's trial. The accused asked what law her adherents had transgressed. Winthrop replied, "the fifth Commandment, which commands us to honour Father and Mother, which includes all in authority, but these seditious practises of theirs, have case reproach and dishonour upon the Fathers of the Commonwealth." There were no Mothers of the Commonwealth. Men designed and controlled the union with Christ. It was only logical, then, that they should see their role vis-a-vis the community as comparable to breast feeding. Winthrop's court addressed the Hutchinsonians in this way: "We beseech you consider, how you should stand in relation to us, as nursing Fathers." The notion reminds one of Hawthorne's vision of the iron-breasted Puritans in "Endicott and the Red Cross." Such nursing, together with

Winthrop's and Cotton's copulation with Christ, had been anticipated by Luther's characterization of preaching as "suckling" and his awaiting Christ *"sicut mulier in conceptu"*— like a woman at the moment of conception. The images recall Bruno Bettelheim's description of men's attempt to assume the processes of generation and nurture in preliterate tribal life.

Lyle Koehler, like Ben Barker-Benfield, is interested in the
sexual dimension of the Antinomian controversy. Koehler's
essay explores that theme by examining Anne Hutchinson
in the context of woman's place and aspirations in New
England in the late 1630s. He contends that Mistress
Hutchinson's protest can best be understood as part of
a more general dissatisfaction of the region's women with
the roles they were relegated to in the brave new world of
the Puritan fathers.

LYLE KOEHLER

"The Case of the American Jezabels"

Between 1636 and 1638 Massachusetts
boiled with controversy, and for more
than three centuries scholars have attempted to define and redefine the
nature, causes, and implications of
that controversy. Commentators have
described the rebellious Antinomians
as "heretics of the worst and most
dangerous sort" who were guilty of
holding "absurd, licentious, and de-
structive" opinions, as "a mob scram-
bling after God, and like all mobs
quickly dispersed once their leaders
were dealt with," and as the innocent
victims of "inexcusable severity and un-

necessary virulence." Other narrators
have called the most famous Antinomian, Anne Hutchinson, a "charismatic
healer, with the gift of fluent and inspired speech," another St. Joan of
Arc, a rebel with a confused, bewildered mind, and a woman "whose stern
and masculine mind . . . triumphed
over the tender affections of a wife
and mother."

Almost without exception, these
critics and defenders of Ms. Hutchinson and the Antinomians have dealt
specifically with Antinomianism as a
religious movement and too little with

it as a social movement. Emery Battis has traced the occupational status of 190 Antinomians and Antinomian sympathizers to examine the secular as well as the religious aspects of the controversy, but his work suffers from one major oversight: only three of his rebels are female. As Richard S. Dunn has rightly observed, "The role of women in colonial life continues to be neglected," and only one colonial specialist, Michael J. Colacurcio, has been much concerned with women as Antinomians. Colacurcio has argued that sexual tensions were central to the Antinomian controversy, but it is not his primary concern to describe the nature of those tensions. Rather, he focuses on Anne Hutchinson as a "type" of Hawthorne's scarlet lady, Hester Prynne. Dunn's appeal, "We need another view of Ms. Hutchinson," still entices.

That Anne Hutchinson and many other Puritan women should at stressful times rebel, either by explicit statement or by implicit example, against the role they were expected to fulfill in society is readily understandable, since that role, in both old and New England, was extremely limiting. The model English woman was weak, submissive, charitable, virtuous, and modest. Her mental and physical activity was limited to keeping the home in order, cooking, and bearing and rearing children, although she might occasionally serve the community as a nurse or midwife. She was urged to avoid books and intellectual exercise, for such activity might overtax her weak mind, and to serve her husband willingly, since she was by nature his inferior. In accordance with the Apostle Pual's doctrine, she was to hold her tongue in church and be careful not "to teach, nor to usurp authority over the man, but to be in silence."

In their letters, lectures, and historical accounts many of the Bay Colony men and some of the women showed approval of modest, obedient, and submissive females. Governor John Winthrop's wife Margaret was careful to leave such important comestic matters as place of residence to her husband's discretion, even when she had a preference of her own. She was ashamed because she felt that she had "no thinge with in or with out" worthy of him and signed her letters to him "your faythfull and obedient wife" or "your lovinge and obedient wife." Lucy Downing, Winthrop's sister, signed her chatty letters to her brother, "Your sister to commaund." Elizabeth, the wife of Winthrop's son John, described herself in a letter to her husband as "thy eaver loveing and kinde wife to comande in whatsoever thou plesest so long as the Lord shall bee plesed to geve me life and strenge."

Winthrop himself was harshly critical of female intellect. In 1645 he wrote that Ann Hopkins, wife of the governor of Connecticut, had lost her understanding and reason by giving herself solely to reading and writing. The Massachusetts statesman commented that if she "had attended her household affairs, and such things as belong to women, and not gone out of her way and calling to meddle in such things as are proper for men, whose minds are stronger, etc. she had kept her wits, and might have improved them usefully and honorably in the place God had set her." Earlier he had denounced Anne Hutchinson as "a woman of a haughty and fierce carriage, of a nimble wit and active spirit, and a very voluble tongue, more bold then a man, though in understanding and judgement, inferiour to many women."

Winthrop echoed the expectations

of the male-dominated society in which he lived, in much the same way as the New England propagandist William Wood and Anne Hutchinson's ministerial accusers did. In 1634 Wood praised the Indian women's "mild carriage and obedience to their husbands," despite his realization that Indian men were guilty of "churlishness and inhumane behavior" toward their wives. Reverend John Cotton arrived in Boston in 1633 and soon requested that women desiring church membership be examined in private since a public confession was "against the apostle's rule and not fit for a women's modesty." At a public lecture less than a year later Cotton explained that the apostle directed women to wear veils in church only when "the custom of the place" considered veils "a sign of the women's subjection." Cambridge minister Thomas Shepard, one of Anne Hutchinson's most severe critics, commended his own wife for her "incomparable meekness of spirit, toward myself especially," while Hugh Peter, a Salem pastor and another of Ms. Hutchinson's accusers, urged his daughter to respect her feminine meekness as "Womans Ornament."

The female role definition that the Massachusetts ministers and magistrates perpetuated severely limited assertiveness, the accomplishment, the independence, and the intellectual activity of Puritan women. Bay Colony women who might resent such a role definition before 1636 had no ideological rationale around which they could organize the expression of their frustration—whatever their consciousness of the causes of that frustration. With the marked increase of Antinomian sentiment in Boston and Anne Hutchinson's powerful example of resistance, the distressed females were able—as this article will attempt to

demonstrate—to channel their frustration into a viable theological form and to rebel openly against the perpetuators of the spiritual and secular status quo. Paradoxically enough, the values that Antinomians embraced minimized the importance of individual action, for they believed that salvation could be demonstrated only by the individual feeling God's grace within.

The process of salvation and the role of the individual in that process was, for the Puritan divines, a matter less well defined. The question of the relative importance of good works (i.e., individual effort) and grace (i.e., God's effort) in preparing man for salvation and concerned English Puritans from their earliest origins, and clergymen of old and New England attempted to walk a broad, although unsure, middle ground between the extremes of Antinomianism and Arminianism. But in 1636 Anne Hutchinson's former mentor and the new teacher of the Boston church, John Cotton, disrupted the fragile theological balance and led the young colony into controversy when he "warned his listeners away from the specious comfort of preparation and re-emphasized the covenant of grace as something in which God acted alone and unassisted." Cotton further explained that a person could become conscious of the dwelling of the Holy Spirit within his soul and directed the Boston congregation "not to be afraid of the word Revelation." The church elders, fearing that Cotton's "Revelation" might be dangerously construed to invalidate biblical law, requested a clarification of his position.

While the elders debated with Cotton the religious issues arising out of his pronouncements, members of Cotton's congregation responded more practically and enthusiastically to the notion of personal revelation by ardently soliciting converts to an emerging, loosely-knit ideology which the divines called pejoratively Antinomianism, Opinionism, or Familism. According to Thomas Weld, fledgling Antinomians visited new migrants to Boston, "especially, men of note, worth, and activity, fit instruments to advance their designe." Antinomian principles were defended at military trainings, in town meetings, and before the court judges. Winthrop charged the Opinionists with causing great disturbance in the church, the state, and the family, and wailed, "All things are turned upside down among us."

The individual hungry for power could, as long as he perceived his deep inner feeling of God's grace to be authentic, use that feeling to consecrate his personal rebellion against the contemporary authorities. Some Boston merchants used it to attack the accretion of political power in the hands of a rural-dominated General Court based on land instead of capital. Some "ignorant and unlettered" men used it to express contempt for the arrogance of "black-coates that have been at the Ninneversity." Some women, as we will see, used it to castigate the authority of the magistrates as guardians of the state, the ministers as guardians of the church, and their husbands as guardians of the home. As the most outspoken of these women, Anne Hutchinson diffused her opinions among all social classes by means of contacts made in the course of her profession of midwifery and in the biweekly teaching sessions she held at her home. Weld believed that Ms. Hutchinson's lectures were responsible for distributing "the venome of these [Antinomian] opinions into the very veines and vitalls of the People in the Country."

Many women identified with Ms. Hutchinson's rebellious intellectual stance and her aggressive spirit. Edward

Johnson wrote that "the weaker Sex" set her up as "a Priest" and "thronged" after her. John Underhill reported he daily heard a "clamor" that "New England men usurp over their wives, and keep them in servile subjection." Winthrop blamed Anne for causing "divisions between husband and wife . . . till the weaker give place to the stronger, otherwise it turnes to open contention," and Weld charged the Antinomians with using the yielding, flexible, and tender women as "an Eve, to catch their husbands also." One anonymous English pamphleteer found in Antinomianism a movement "somewhat like the Trojan horse for rarity" because "it was covered with womens aprons, and bolstered out with the judgement and deep discerning of the godly and reverent."

From late 1636 through early 1637 female resistance in the Boston church reached its highest pitch. At one point, when pastor John Wilson rose to preach, Ms. Hutchinson left the congregation and many women followed her out of the meetinghouse. These women "pretended many excuses for their going out," an action which made it impossible for the authorities to convict them of contempt for Wilson. Other rebels did, however, challenge Wilson's words as he spoke them, causing Weld to comment, "Now the faithfull Ministers of Christ must have dung cast on their faces, and be no better than Legall Preachers, Baals Priests, Popish Factors, Scribes, Pharisees, and Opposers of Christ himselfe."

Included among these church rebels were two particularly active women, Jane (Mrs. Richard) Hawkins and milliner William Dyer's wife Mary, both of whom Winthrop found obnoxious. The governor considered the youthful Ms. Dyer to be "of a very proud spirit," "much addicted to revelations," and "notoriously infected with Mrs. Hutchinson's errors." Ms. Dyer weathered Winthrop's wrath and followed Anne to Rhode Island, but her "addictions" were not without serious consequence. Twenty-two years later she would return to Boston and be hanged as a Quaker. The other of Hutchinson's close female associates, Jane Hawkins, dispensed fertility potions to barren women and occasionally fell into a trance-like state in which she spoke Latin. Winthrop therefore denounced her as "notorious for familiarity with the devill," and the General Court, sharing his apprehension, on March 12, 1638, forbade her to question "matters of religion" or "to meddle" in "surgery, or phisick, drinks, plaisters, or oyles." Ms. Hawkins apparently disobeyed this order, for three years later the Court banished her from the colony under the penalty of a severe whipping or such other punishment as the judges thought fit.

Other women, both rich and poor, involved themselves in the Antinomian struggle. William Coddington's spouse, like her merchant husband, was "taken with the familistical opinions." Mary Dummer, the wife of wealthy landowner and Assistant Richard Dummer, convinced her husband to move from Newbury to Boston so that she might be closer to Ms. Hutchinson. Mary Oliver, a poor Salem calenderer's wife, reportedly exceeded Anne "for ability of speech, and appearance of zeal and devotion" and, according to Winthrop, might "have done hurt, but that she was poor and had little acquaintance [with theology]." Ms. Oliver held the "dangerous" opinions that the church was managed by the "heads of the people, both magistrates and ministers, met together," instead of the people themselves, and that anyone professing faith in Christ ought to be admitted to the church and the sacraments. Between 1638 and 1650 she appeared before the magistrates six times for remarks contemptuous of ministerial and magisterial authority and experienced the stocks, the lash, the placement of a cleft stick on her tongue, and imprisonment. One of the Salem magistrates became so frustrated with Ms. Oliver's refusal to respect his authority that he seized her and put her in the stocks without a trial. She sued him for false arrest and collected a minimal ten shillings in damages. Her victory was short-lived, however, and before she left Massachusetts in 1650 she had managed to secure herself some reputation as a witch.

Mary Oliver and the other female rebels could easily identify with the Antinomian ideology because its theological emphasis on the inability of the individual to achieve salvation echoed the inability of women to achieve recognition on a sociopolitical level. As the woman realized that she could receive wealth, power, and status only through the man, her father or her husband, so the Antinomian realized that he or she could receive grace only through God's beneficence. Thus, women could have found it appealing that in Antinomianism *both* men and women were relegated vis-à-vis God to the status that women occupied in Puritan society vis-à-vis men, that is, to the status of malleable inferiors in the hands of a higher being. All power, then, emanated from God, raw and pure, respecting no sex, rather than from male authority figures striving to interpret the Divine Word. Fortified by a consciousness of the Holy Spirit's inward dwelling, the Antinomians could rest secure and self-confident in the belief that they were mystic participants in the trancendent power of the Almighty, a power far beyond anything mere magistrates and ministers might muster. Antinomianism could not secure for women such practical earthly powers as sizable estates, professional success, and participation in the church and civil government, but it provided compensation by reducing the significance of these powers for the men. Viewed from this perspective, Antinomianism extended the feminine experience of humility to both sexes, which in turn paradoxically created the possibility of feminine pride, as Anne Hutchinson's dynamic example in her examinations and trials amply demonstrated.

Anne Hutchinson's example caused the divines much frustration. They were chagrined to find that she was not content simply to repeat to the "simple Weomen" the sermons of John Wilson, but that she also chose to interpret and even question the content of those sermons. When she charged that the Bay Colony ministers did not teach a covenant of grace as "Clearly" as Cotton and her brother-in-law, John Wheelwright, she was summoned in 1636 to appear before a convocation of the clergy. At this convocation and in succeeding examinations, the ministers found particularly galling her implicit assertion that she had the intellectual ability necessary to judge the truth of their theology. Such an assertion threatened their self-image as the intellectual leaders of the community and the spokesmen for a male-dominated society. The ministers and magistrates therefore sharply criticized Anne for not fulfilling her ordained womanly role. In September 1637 a synod of elders resolved that women might meet "to pray and edify one another," but when one woman "in a prophetical way" resolved questions of doctrine and expounded Scripture, then the meeting was "disorderly." At Anne's examination on November 7 and 8,

Winthrop began the interrogation by charging that she criticized the ministers and maintained a "meeting and an assembly in your house that hath been condemned by the general assembly as a thing not tolerable nor comely in the sight of God nor fitting for your sex." Later in the interrogation, Winthrop accused her of disobeying her "parents," the magistrates, in violation of the Fifth Commandment, and paternalistically told her, "We do not mean to discourse with those of your sex." Hugh Peter also indicated that he felt Anne was not fulfilling the properly submissive, nonintellectual feminine role. He ridiculed her choice of a female preacher of the Isle of Ely as a model for her own behavior and told her to consider "that you have stept out of you place, *you have rather bine a Husband than a Wife and a preacher than a Hearer; and a Magistrate than a Subject."*

When attacked for behavior inappropriate to her sex, Ms. Hutchinson did not hesitate to demonstrate that she was the intellectual equal of her accusers. She tried to trap Winthrop when he charged her with dishonoring her "parents": "But put the case Sir that I do fear the Lord and my parents, may not I entertain them that fear the Lord because my parents will not give me leave?" To provide a biblical justification for her teaching activities, she cited Titus's rule (2:3-4) "that the elder women should instruct the younger." Winthrop ordered her to take that rule "in the sense that elder women must instruct the younger about their business, and to love their husbands." But Anne disagreed with this interpretation, saying, "I do not conceive but that it is meant for some publick times." Winthrop rejoined, "We must . . . restrain you from maintaining this course," and she qualified, "If you have a rule for it from God's word you may." Her resistance infuriated the governor, who exclaimed, "We are your judges, and not you ours." When Winthrop tried to lure her into admitting that she taught men, in violation of Paul's proscription, Anne replied that she throught herself justified in teaching a man who asked her for instruction, and added sarcastically, "Do you think it not lawful for me to teach women and why do you call me to teach the court?"

• • •

Anne, although aware of the "backwardness" of women as a group, did not look to intensified group activity as a remedy for woman's downtrodden status. Her feminism consisted essentially of the subjective recognition of her own strength and gifts and the apparent belief that other women could come to the same recognition. A strong, heroic example of female self-assertiveness was necessary to the development of this recognition of one's own personal strength. Anne chose the woman preacher of the Isle of Ely as her particular heroic model; she did, Hught Peter chided, "exceedingly magnifie" that woman "to be a Womane of 1000 hardly any like to her." Anne could thus dissociate herself from the "divers worthy and godly Weomen" of Massachusetts and confidently deride them as being no better than "soe many Jewes," unconverted by the light of Christ. Other Bay Colony women who wished to reach beyond the conventional, stereotypic behavior of "worthy and godly Weomen" attached themselves to the emphatic example of Anne and to God's ultimate power in order to resist the constraints which they felt as Puritan women.

Fearful that Ms. Hutchinson's example might be imitated by other women, the divines wished to catch her in a major theological error and subject her to public punishment. Their efforts were not immediately successful. Throughout her 1637 examination Anne managed to parry the verbal thrusts of the ministers and magistrates by replying to their many questions with questions of her own, forcing them to justify their positions from the Bible, pointing out their logical inconsistencies, and using innuendo to cast aspersions upon their authoritarianism. With crucial assistance from a sympathetic John Cotton, she left the ministers with no charge to pin upon her. She was winning the debate when, in an apparently incautious moment, she gave the authorities the kind of declaration for which they had been hoping. Raising herself to the position of judge over her accusers, she asserted, "I know that for this you goe about to doe to me, God will ruine you and your posterity, and this whole State." Asked how she knew this, she explained, "By an immediate revelation." With this statement Anne proved her heresy to the ministers and they then took steps to expose her in excommunication proceedings conducted before the Boston church. The divines hoped to expel a heretic from their midst, to reestablish support for the Puritan way, to prevent unrest in the state and the family, and to shore up their own anxious egos in the process.

The predisposition of the ministers to defame Ms. Hutchinson before the congregation caused them to ignore what she was actually saying in her excommunication trial. Although she did describe a relationship with Christ closer than anything Cotton had envisioned, she did not believe that she had experienced Christ's Second Coming in her own life. Such a claim would have denied the resurrection of the body at the Last Judgment and would have clearly stamped her as a Familist. Ms. Hutchinson's accusers, ignoring Thomas Leverett's reminder that she had expressed belief in the resurrection, argued that if the resurrection did not exist, biblical law would have no validity nor the marriage covenant any legal or utilitarian value. The result would be a kind of world no Puritan could tolerate, a world where the basest desires would be fulfilled and "foule, groce, filthye and abominable" sexual promiscuity would be rampant. Cotton, smarting from a psychological slap Anne had given him earlier in the excommunication proceedings and in danger of losing the respect of the other ministers, admonished her with the words "though I have not herd, nayther do I thinke, you have bine unfaythfull to your Husband in his Marriage Covenant, *yet that will follow upon it.*" By referring to "his" marriage covenant Cotton did not even accord Anne equal participation in the making of that covenant. The Boston teacher concluded his admonition with a criticism of Anne's pride: "*I have often feared the highth of your Spirit and being puft up with your owne parts.*"

Both the introduction of the sexual issue into the trial and Cotton's denunciation of Ms. Hutchinson must have had the effect of curbing dissent from the congregation. Few Puritans would want to defend Anne in public when such a defense could be construed as supporting promiscuity. Since Cotton had earlier been sympathetic to the Antinomian cause and had tried to save Anne at her 1637 examination, his vigorous condemnation of her must have confused her following. Cotton even went so far as to exempt the male Antinomians from any real blame for the controversy when he characterized Antinomianism as a women's delusion. He urged that

women, like children, ought to be watched, reproved Hutchinson's sons for not controlling her theological ventures, and called those sons "Vipers . . . [who] *Eate through the very Bowells of your Mother*, to her Ruine." Cotton warned the Boston women "to looke to your selves and to take heed that you reaceve nothinge for Truth which hath not the stamp of the Word of God [as interpreted by the ministers] . . . for you see she [Anne] is but a Woman and *many unsound and dayngerous principles are held by her.*" Thomas Shepard agreed that intellectual activity did not suit women and worned the congregation that Anne was likely "to seduce and draw away many, Espetially simple Weomen of her owne sex."

The female churchmembers, who would have had good reason to resent the clergy's approach, could not legitimately object to the excommunication proceedings because of Paul's injunction against women speaking in church. Lacking a clearly-defined feminist consciousness and filled with "backward" fear, the women could not refuse to respect that injunction, even though, or perhaps because, Anne had been presented to the congregation as the epitome of despicableness, as a woman of simple intellect, and as a liar, puffed up with pride and verging on sexual promiscuity. This caricature of Anne did not, however, prevent five men, including her brother-in-law Richard Scott and Mary Oliver's husband Thomas, from objecting to her admonition and excommunication. Cotton refused to consider the points these men raised and dismissed their objections as rising out of their own self-interest or their natural affection for Anne.

• • •

During the year and a half following

Ms. Hutchinson's excommunication, the Massachusetts ministers and magistrates prosecuted several other female rebels. In April 1638 the Boston church cast out Judith Smith, the maidservant of Anne's brother-in-law, Edward Hutchinson, for her "obstinate persisting" in "sundry Errors." On October 10 of the same year the Assistants ordered Katherine Finch to be whipped for "speaking against the magistrates, against the Churches, and against the Elders." Less than a year later Ms. Finch again appeared before the Assistants, this time for not carrying herself "dutifully to her husband," and was released upon promise of reformation. In September 1639 the Boston church excommunicated Phillip(a?) Hammond "as a slaunderer and revyler both of the Church and Common Weale." Ms. Hammond, after her husband's death, had resumed her maiden name, operated a business in Boston, and argued in her shop and at public meetings "that Mrs. Hutchinson neyther deserved the Censure which was putt upon her in the Church, nor in the Common Weale." The Boston church also excommunicated two other women for partially imitating Anne Hutchinson's example: Sarah Keayne was found guilty in 1646 of "irregular prophesying in mixed assemblies," and Joan Hogg nine years later was punished "for her disorderly singing and her idleness, and for saying she is commanded of Christ so to do."

The Salem authorities followed Boston's example in dealing with overly assertive women. In late 1638 the Salem church excommunicated four of Roger Williams's former followers: Jane (Mrs. Joshua) Verin, Mary Oliver, servant Margery Holliman, and widow Margery Reeves. These women had consistently refused to worship with the congregation, and the latter

two had denied that the churches of the Bay Colony were true churches. Yet another woman, Dorothy Talby, who was subject to a different kind of frustation, troubled the Essex County magistrates by mimicking Anne Hutchinson's proclamation of "immediate revelation" to justify her personal rebellion. In October 1637 the county court ordered her chained to a post "for frequent laying hands on her husband to the danger of his life, and contemning the authority of the court," and later ordered her whipped for "misdemeanors against her husband." Later, according to Winthrop, she claimed a "revelation from heaven" instructing her to kill her husband and children and then broke the neck of her three-year-old daughter, Difficult. At her execution on December 6, 1638, Ms. Talby continued her defiance by refusing to keep her face covered and expressing a desire to be beheaded, as "it was less painful and less shameful."

Dorothy Talby was one of an increasing number of women to appear before the General Court and the Court of Assistants, an increase which seemed to reflect both a greater rebelliousness in women and a hardening of magisterial attitudes. In the first five years of Puritan settlement only 1.7 percent of the persons convicted of criminal offenses by the Deputies and the Assistants were women. During and after the years of the Antinomian controversy the percentage of female offenders was significantly higher— 6.7 percent from 1635 to 1639 and 9.4 percent from 1640 to 1644. If Charles E. Banks's enumeration of 3,505 passengers from ship lists is representative of the more than 20,000 persons who came to Massachusetts between 1630 and 1639, it can be assumed that the number of women did not increase proportionately to

he number of men. Banks's ship lists
eveal that 829 males and 542 females
ame to Massachusetts between 1630
nd 1634, a number which increased
n the next five years to 1,279 males
nd 855 females. The percentage of
emales increased only .6 percent,
rom 39.5 percent between 1630 and
1634 to 40.1 percent between 1635
nd 1639. These comparative figures
uggest that by 1640 the magistrates
:ould no longer afford to dismiss with
verbal chastisement females found
guilty of drunkenness, cursing, or
premarital fornication.

• • •

Besides prosecuting Antinomian
sympathizers in church and court, the
Massachusetts ministers and magistrates carefully watched new ministers, lest they deliver "some points
savoring of familism," and justified
the emergent orthodox position in
their sermons and publications. Of
these publications, which were directed at audiences both in New and
old England, John Cotton's *Singing
of Psalmes a Gospel-Ordinance* most
significantly asserted the traditional
feminine role-response. The Boston
teacher, apparently with Ms. Hutchinson in mind, told his readers that
"the woman is more subject to error
than a man" and continued, "It is not
permitted to a woman to speak in the
Church by way of propounding questions though under pretence of desire
to learn for her own satisfaction; but
rather it is required she should ask
her husband at home. For under pretence of questioning for learning sake,
she might so propound her question
as to teach her teachers; or if not so,
yet to open a door to some of her
own weak and erroneous apprehensions, or at least soon exceed the
bounds of womanly modesty." Cotton
explained that a woman could speak
in church only when she wished to
confess a sin or to participate in singing hymns.

Other Bay Colony leaders popu-
larized the idea that the intellectual
woman was influenced by Satan and
was therefore unable to perform the
necessary functions of womanhood.
Weld described Mary Dyer's abortive
birth as "a woman child, a fish, a
beast, and a fowle, all woven together
in one, and without an head," and
wrote of Anne Hutchinson's probable
hydatidiform mole as "30. monstrous
births . . . none at all of them (as farre
as I could ever learne) of humane
shape." According to Winthrop's even
more garish account of Mary Dyer's
child, the stillborn baby had a face
and ears growing upon the shoulders,
a breast and back full of sharp prickles,
female sex organs on the rear and but-
tocks in front, three clawed feet, no
forehead, four horns above the eyes,
and two great holes upon the back.

• • •

Despite Wheelwright's effort, Weld's
opinion that "as she had vented mis-
shapen opinions, so she must bring
forth deformed monsters" impressed
the people of the Bay Colony, a people
who believed that catastrophic occur-
rences were evidences of God's displeasure. Some Massachusetts residents viewed the births as the products
of both the women's "mishapen opinions" and their supposed promiscuity.
Edward Johnson and Roger Clap la-
mented the "phantasticall madnesse"
of those who would hold "silly women
laden with their lusts" in higher esteem
than "those honoured of Christ, indued
with power and authority from him
to Preach."

• • •

The effort to discredit the Antinomians and Antinomian sentiment in the
Bay Colony was quite successful. By
the late 1640s Antinomianism, in a
practical sense, was no longer threat-

ening; the ministers and magistrates had managed to preserve a theological system they found congenial. *"Sanctification* came to be in some Request again; and there were *Notes* and *Marks* given of a good Estate." The position of Massachusetts women within the religious system remained essentially unchanged, while in Rhode Island and nearby Providence Plantations the status of women was somewhat improved. In Providence and Portsmouth the men listened to the wishes of the women and protected the "liberty" of women to teach, preach, and attend services of their choosing. When Joshua Verin, one of the original settlers at Providence, restrained his wife Jane from attending religious services at Roger Williams's home, a town meeting considered the matter. John Greene argued before the townsmen that if men were allowed to restrain their wives, "all the women in the country would cry out." William Arnold rejoined that God had ordered the wife to be subject to her husband and that such a commandment should not be broken merely to please women. According to Winthrop, the townsmen "would have censured Verin, [but] Arnold told them, that it was against their own order, for Verin did that he did out of conscience; and their order was, that no man should be censured for his conscience." Winthrop neglected to record that the town meeting did disfranchise Verin until he declared that he would not restrain his wife's "libertie of conscience," nor did Winthrop mention that Verin had "trodden" his wife "under foot tyrantically and brutishly" endandering her life.

• • •

Willaim Hutchinson died at Newport in 1640, and for much of that year Anne was silent. By 1641, however, she had come out of mourning and,

according to Winthrop, turned anabaptist. She and "divers" others supported passive resistance to authority, "denied all magistracy among Christians, and maintained that there were no churches since those founded by the apostles and evangelists, nor could any be." Such opinions achieved enough popularity in Rhode Island to contribute to the dissolution of the church at Newport, although not enough to remove Coddington from power. Disgruntled and fearing that Massachusetts would seize the Rhode Island settlements, Anne sought refuge in the colony of New Netherland in 1642, but her stay there was not long. In August 1643 she, William Collins, two of her sons, and three of her daughters were killed by Indians who had quarreled with her Dutch neighbors.

• • •

The Bay Colony divines considered Anne Hutchinson's death to be the symbolic death of Antinomianism. To these divines she had been the incarnation of the Antinomian evil, and their accounts of the Antinomian stress in Boston accented *her* beliefs, *her* activities, and *her* rebelliousness. The ministers were not as concerned with the important roles played by Coddington, Wheelwright, Vane, and the other male Antinomian leaders because none of these men threatened the power and status structure of society in the concrete way that Anne Hutchinson did. Anne was clearly not, as the ministers might have wished, a submissive quiet dove, content to labor simply in the kitchen and the childbed. She was witty, aggressive, and intellectual. She had no qualms about castigating in public the men who occupied the most authoritative positions. She claimed the right to define rational, theological matters for herself and by her example spurred ther women to express a similar demand. Far from bewildered, she thwarted her accusers with her intellectual ability. Perceiving her as a threat to the family, the state, the religion, and the status hierarchy, the Puritan authorities directed their antagonism against Anne's character and her sex. By doing so, they managed to salve the psychological wounds inflicted by this woman who trod so sharply upon their male status and their ministerial and magisterial authority. Their method had a practical aspect as well; it helped restore respect for the ministry and curb potential dissent.

Anne's ability to attract large numbers of women as supporters caused the ministers and magistrates some worry but little surprise, since they believed that women were easily deluded. They chided Anne for choosing a female preacher as a role model and refused to attribute any merit to her at times subtle, at times caustic intellectual ability. They could see only the work of Satan in Anne's aggressiveness and not the more human desire for equal opportunity and treatment which this rebel never hesitated to assert by example in the intellectual skirmishes she had with her accusers throughout her trials. The double oppression of life in a male-dominated society, combined with biological bondage to her own amazing fertility, could not destroy her self-respect. Because of the theologically based society in which she lived, it was easy for her to ally herself with God and to express her self-confidence in religious debates with the leading intellectual authorities. Neither Anne's rebellion nor the rebellion of her female followers was directed self-consciously against their collective female situation or toward its improvement. Specific feminist campaigns for the franchise, divorce reform, female property ownership after marriage, and the like would be developments of a much later era. For Anne Hutchinson and her female associates Antinomianism was simply an ideology through which the resentments they intuitively felt could be focused and actively expressed.

When Nathaniel Hawthorne directed his imagination to his Puritan ancestors he came closer to understanding their beliefs and behavior than many historians who have written of early New England. Knowledge of the history of Massachusetts and sympathy for the people who lived that history permeates many of his works, particularly *The Scarlet Letter*. In this article Michael Colacurcio examines Hawthorne's short work on Anne Hutchinson in order to gain insight into *The Scarlet Letter*. In the process he also illuminates new aspects of what Hawthorne perceived to be the sexual dimension of the conflict surrounding Anne Hutchinson.

MICHAEL COLACURCIO
"Footsteps of Anne Hutchinson"

In the first brief chapter of *The Scarlet Letter*, the narrator pays almost as much attention to a rose bush as he does to the appearance and moral significance of Puritan America's first prison. . . . Accordingly, criticism has been lavish in its own attention to that rose bush: it has, out of perfect soundness of instinct, been made the starting point of more than one excellent reading of *The Scarlet Letter*; indeed the explication of this image and symbol is one of the triumphs of the "new" Hawthorne criticism.

But if the "natural" and internal associations of this rose bush have been successfully elaborated, its external and "historic" implications have been largely ignored. And yet not for any fault of the narrator. This rose bush "has been kept alive in history," he assures us; and it may even be, as "there is fair authority for believing," that "it had sprung up under the footsteps of the sainted Ann Hutchinson, as she entered the prison-door."

• • •

We should not, it seems to me, want to believe Hawthorne a casual name dropper unless he prove himself one.

We should prefer a more rather than a less precise use of literary allusion, not only in this opening reference but also in a later one which suggests that, except for the existence of Pearl, Hester "might have come down to us in history, hand in hand with Ann Hutchinson, as the foundress of a religious sect" (165). The references are, after all, pretty precise: Hester walks in the footsteps of (but not quite hand-in-hand with) Ann Hutchinson. . . . We might remind ourselves that Hawthorne did write—near the outset of his career, in clear and close dependence on "a good many books" —a well informed sketch called "Mrs. Hutchinson." He mentions her again, prominently, in those reviews of New England history entitled *Grandfather's Chair* and "Main Street." Now he seems to be apprising us of a relationship between Hester Prynne and that famous lady heretic. The man who created the one and memorialized the other ought to be in a position to know.

Clearly the relationship is not one of "identity": tempting as the view can be made to appear, *The Scarlet Letter* is probably not intended as an allegory of New England's Antinomian Crisis. Hawthorne's historical tales never work quite that simply: . . . However "antinomian" Hester becomes, it would be positively ludicrous to forget that her philosophical career is inseparable from adultery and illegitimate childbirth, events which have no very real counterpart in the life of that enthusiastic prophetess Hawthorne calls her prototype.

But as important as are the simple differences, and as dangerous as it must always seem to turn away from the richness and particularity of Hester's own love story. Hawthorne himself seems to have invited us temporarily to do so. And if we follow his suggestion, a number of similarities come teasingly to mind.

Like Ann Hutchinson, Hester Prynne is an extraordinary woman who falls afoul of a theocratic and male-dominated society; and the problems which cause them to be singled out for exemplary punishment both begin in a special sort of relationship with a pastor who is one of the acknowledged intellectual and spiritual leaders of that society. No overt sexual irregularity seems to have been associated with Mrs. Hutchinson's denial that converted saints were under the moral law, but (as we shall see later) no one could read what seventeenth-century Puritan observers said about the "seductiveness" of her doctrines without sensing sexual implications everywhere. Evidently such implications were not lost on Hawthorne. Further, though with increasing complications, both of these remarkable and troublesome women have careers as nurses and counsellors to other women: Ann Hutchinson begins her prophetic career this way, whereas Hester Prynne moves in this direction as a result of her punishment. And most significantly— if most problematically—both make positive pronouncements about the inapplicability of what the majority of their contemporaries take to be inviolable moral law.

To be sure, it takes Hester Prynne some time to catch up with Ann Hutchinson; but when Hawthorne says of Hester, in the full tide of her later speculative freedom, that "the world's law was no law to her mind" (164), we may well suspect that he intends some conscious pun on the literal meaning of "antinomianism." If Hester's problems begin with sex more literally than do Ann Hutchinson's, her thinking eventually ranges far outward from that domestic subject. In some way, and for complicated reasons that need to be examined, Hester Prynne and sex are associated in Hawthorne's mind with Ann Hutchinson and spiritual freedom.

So teasing do Hawthorne's connections and analogies come to seem, that we are eventually led to wonder whether *The Scarlet Letter* shows only this one set of historical footprints. If Hester Prynne bears relation to Ann Hutchinson, would it be too outrageous to look for similarities between Arthur Dimmesdale and John Cotton, that high Calvinist who was variously asserted and denied to be the partner in heresy? And—granting that what is involved is neither allegory nor *roman à clef*—might there not be some fundamental relation between the deepest philosophical and theological "issues" raised by the Antinomian Controversy and the "themes" of Hawthorne's romance?

To the first of these questions, a certain kind of answer comes readily enough. Although the portrait of Dimmesdale is physically unlike the one Hawthorne gives of Cotton in his early sketch of "Mrs. Hutchinson," their positions are disturbingly similar: both are singled out from among distinguished colleagues as models of learning and piety: and both relate very ambiguously to a wayward woman on trial. It is impossible not to feel that John Cotton's drastic change of relation to Ann Hutchinson—a phenomenon as fascinating to scholars now as it was momentous to Puritans then—lies somewhere behind Dimmesdale's movement from partner in to judge of Hester's adultery. Both men sit in public judgment of an outrage against public order in which there is reason to believe they bear equal responsibility with the criminal.

Although his sketch of "Mrs. Hutchinson" suggests in one place that her enthusiasm had earlier been restrained from public manifestation by the influence of her favorite pastor, Hawthorne actually takes a rather harsh view of Cotton's role in her trial: "Mr. Cotton began to have that light in regard to her errors, which will sometimes break in upon the wisest and most pious men, when their opinions are unhappily discordant with those of the powers that be" (XII, 222). That is to say: Cotton and his female parishioner have been what their society calls "antinomians" together, both "deceived by the fire" (221): but the respected minister saves himself. Not all modern commentators would agree that Cotton's behavior is to be judged this harshly, but that is not the issue here. At some point Cotton did clearly reverse his relationship to Ann Hutchinson, reproving doctrines she thought were his own offspring; and clearly Hawthorne's view of Cotton has influenced his treatment of Dimmesdale. Except for the rather too delicate question of who first lit the strange fires, both Mrs. Hutchinson's treatment by Cotton and Hester's by Dimmesdale might almost be subtitled "Seduced and Abandoned in Old Boston."

Although the significance is completely ironic in *The Scarlet Letter*, both pastors are reminded by their colleagues that "the responsibility of [the] woman's soul" is largely within their sphere; Wilson's urging Dimmesdale to press repentence and confession upon Hester sounds a good deal like an ironic version of the ministerial pleas which Cotton, because of his doctrinal affinities with Ann Hutchinson, so long refused to heed. And to the end, both men are spared from denunciation by their partners. Although Puritan defenders of Cotton's doctrinal reputation (like Cotton Mather) insisted he had been slandered by even being named in the same breath with

he seductive Mrs. Hutchinson, there
s no evidence to suggest that the
"abandoned" one ever pointed a finger of public accusation at Cotton, or
reproached him for infidelity to what
she continued to believe were their
shared experiences and beliefs. Cotton
alone, Hawthorne reports, is excepted
from her final denunciations. And in
spite of Dimmesdale's false and un-
faithful position on the balcony over-
looking her scaffold, of his own part
in her troubles, Hester "will not
speak."

• • •

In the public judgment of Hester,
Dimmesdale stands as the partner of
John Wilson, at the head of the Boston
church of which Hester is a member:
Wilson is the fervent, Dimmesdale the
reluctant enforcer of discipline. Now
it seems to me inconceivable that the
man who wrote about the Hutchinson
situation explicitly three separate
times, using highly detailed contemporary sources as well as later histories
(and who built into *The Scarlet Letter*
certain colonial details so minutely accurate as to convince one recent critic
that he wrote the romance with a
number of books open before him)
would *not* know that the famous
partnership at Boston throughout the
1630's and 1640's was Wilson and
Cotton. It might be too much to suggest that Dimmesdale is conceived and
dramatized as a younger version of
Cotton, one whose pastoral involve-
ment with Hester Prynne amounted
to a less metaphorical seduction than
Cotton's relationship with Ann Hutchinson; but it is hard to believe Hawthorne could pair Wilson with *Dimmesdale* without thinking *Cotton*.

Several other, more curious "dis-
placements" also implicate Cotton.
Hawthorne had certainly read in
Mather's *Magnalia* of a case in which
John Wilson and John Cotton joined

together publicly to urge public repentance upon a woman who had
killed an illegitimate child; Mather's
account surely lies somewhere behind
Hawthorne's first scaffold scene. Also
he could scarcely have *not* known that
it was with Cotton's death in 1652
that the fiery signs in the sky were
associated—not with Winthrop's in
1649. One could argue, of course, that
this points *away* from Cotton; but just
as cogently one can say that Hawthorne
cannot *make* the transference without
having Cotton in mind; and that the
reader who knows the facts will make
the application, especially when, standing on his midnight scaffold, Dimmesdale applies "Cotton's" sign to himself.
And finally, it was not exactly a secret
(despite Mather's silence) that Cotton's
son, John Cotton, *Junior*, was deprived
of his pastorship and excommunicated
from church membership at Plymouth
for adultery. Perhaps Dimmesdale is
to be thought of—metaphorically, and
with a certain irony—as a sort of offspring of Cotton's principles.

• • •

The place to begin an exploration
of the inner similarities between Hester Prynne and Ann Hutchinson is
with a closer look at Hawthorne's
early sketch. In many ways a puzzling
piece of historical fiction, the sketch
does clear up one fundamental point
immediately: Hester's sexual problems
can be related to those of Mrs. Hutchinson because the latter are, in Hawthorne's view, themselves flagrantly
sexual.

• • •

Once we apprehend Hawthorne's dominant image of Ann Hutchinson—
formerly a spiritual counsellor to
Puritan women, interpreting to them
the best of the male theological mind;
now a prophet in her own right, giving
voice to a new spirit of freedom and
embodying within herself a new aware-

ness of female intelligence and social power—we immediately grasp the significant context of Hawthorne's views of the later Hester Prynne.

In the epilogue which Hawthorne calls a "Conclusion," Hester has returned to Boston to wear her scarlet letter "of her own free will," with something like an internalized acceptance of its appropriateness. She now accepts as reasonable what in the forest she tried to deny and many years earlier she could, in very much the same words, only rationalize: "Here had been her sin; here, her sorrow; and here was yet to be her penitence" (263). But this is not the whole story. Whether to affirm a yet undestroyed inner-direction and unreconstructed self-reliance, or else to assert once again the mortal irreparability of ruined walls, the narrator informs us that Hester is still a visionary and has become a counsellor to women. Earlier—even in her most antinomian moments—she had stopped short of that critical move from undisciplined private speculation to unsanctioned public prophecy; providentially she had been prevented from joining hands (metaphorically) with her sister Hutchinson because "in the education of the child, the mother's enthusiasm of thought had something to weak itself upon" (165). Now, although Hester has apparently picked up and pieced together again "the fragments of [the] broken chain" formerly cast away; although "the world's law" is now apparently *some* law to her mind; and although she would not now presumably claim for her adultery a totally sufficient "consecration" in feeling, she has now found a way to make public her ideas about sexual justice.

Earlier she had pondered the "dark question" of the "whole race of womanhood": could its lot ever be a happy one without a tearing down of "the whole system of society" and an essential modification of "the very nature of the opposite sex" (165)? Now—with important modifications of tone and in separation from all traces of antinomian self-justification —her ideas are expressed to other women, especially those whose lives have been made miserable through excess or absence of passion.

> Hester comforted and counseled them, as best she might. She assured them, too, of her firm belief, that, at some brighter period, when the world should have grown ripe for it, in Heaven's own time, a new truth would be revealed, in order to establish the whole relation between man and woman on a surer ground of mutual happiness. (263)

What Hester's experience comes to finally—in an epilogue, and after a painful and complicated development forced upon her by others—is some insight about the double standard, or perhaps about the new morality.

Thus, if we can bear the temporary critical reduction, it is easy to see that Hester passes through a phase of antinomianism comparable to (though not identical with) that of the historical Ann Hutchinson, only to emerge as a version of the sexual reformer already "typed out" in Hawthorne's "figure" of Mrs. Hutchinson as independent and reforming "female." And though the equation might need to be clarified by an examination of the precise quality of Hester's anti-legal phase, we can already calculate that her final position is, in Hawthorne's mental universe, just about half way between Ann Hutchinson and Margaret Fuller; and we can sense that when Hawthorne describes her later career as counsellor to troubled and searching women, he has certain seventeenth-century, Sunday-evening doctrinal meetings and

certain nineteenth-century "Conversations" just about equally in mind.

• • •

To this point, as I have indicated.
Hawthorne seems open to the charge
of a fairly radical sort of reductivism:
he seems to have presented an historical woman whose heretical ideas once
caused a profound religious and social
crisis as a simple case of uneasy or
misplaced sexuality; and the opportunity to reduce Hester Prynne to a
woman whose sexuality got quite
literally out of control and never did
entirely recover itself is therefore
ready to hand. Such a reduction is, presumably, as distasteful to old male
literary critics as it is to new women.

• • •

If we glance again at the early
sketch, we can notice that, embattled
and argumentative as it is, it is yet
about sex in some more elemental
way than our discussion about "feminism" has so far indicated. With struc-
tural intention (and not, clearly, by
obsession), the sketch tries hard to
focus on several scenes in which Mrs.
Hutchinson is the center of all male
attention, prophesying doctrines that
astound the male intellect. Most of
the "historical" facts are there, but
only a fairly well informed reader can
feel assured of this; and except for an
initial, one-paragraph reminder, the
facts seem to fall out incidentally, so
as not to distract from the dramatic
confrontation. The implications, in
turn, are not in the ordinary sense
"theological": there is no mention of
the famous eighty-two errors Mrs.
Hutchinson is said to have spawned—
as there is, self-consciously, in *Grandfather's Chair*; we are, historically and
psychologically, beyond that sort of
consideration. The issue is not sanctification as an evidence of justification,
but the woman's own prophetic abilities. Having formerly cast aspersions on

legal doctrines of salvation, the enthusiast now claims the spiritual "power
of distinguishing between the chosen
of man and the sealed of heaven"(XII,
224). What further need of witnesses?
Clearly the progress of the strange fire
of her enthusiasm is far advanced.

Nor is there any significant ambiguity about the source and significance
of that fire: Mrs. Hutchinson's spiritual
openings and leadings are inseparable
from her female sexuality. Although
her "dark enthusiasm" has deceived
the impetuous Vane and the learned
but mildly illuministic Cotton, it is
clearly her own "strange fire now laid
upon the altar" (XII, 221). The men,
variously affected, must make of it
whatever they can. Hawthorne does
not quite identify enthusiasm with
"the female," but we do not distort
his intentions if—supplying our own
italics—we take as the very heart of
the sketch the following sentence:
"In the midst, and in the center of all
eyes, we see *the woman*" (XII, 224).

This may still be sexist, but it is no
longer petty or carping. Mrs. Hutchinson's influence is indeed profound.
Even the male chauvinist is compelled
to admit it. The impulse to challenge
the Puritan theocracy's dominant (and
socially conservative) assumptions
about "visible sanctity" evidently
comes from a fairly deep and powerful
source. It seems to be coming from—
"the woman."

Evidently, in Hawthorne's view,
fully awakened women accept the inevitability of a given legal order far less
easily than their male counterparts.
And clearly this is the central issue.
What caused a state of near civil war
in Boston and what creates the crack-
ling tension in Hawthorne's sketch is
Mrs. Hutchinson's proclamation—
variously worded at various times, but
always as far beyond the reach of the
"trained and sharpened intellects" of

the most scholastic Puritan contro-
versialists as are Hester Prynne's
sexual secrets—that "the chosen of
man" are not necessarily "the sealed
of heaven." Here, in her last, most
devastating, and for Hawthorne most
insupportable formulation, Mrs.
Hutchinson is claiming that sort of
direct inspiration and divine guidance
necessary to distinguish between true
and false, spiritual and legal teachers.
But she has been forced to this last
claim by the pressure of investigation
and over-response; this, presumably,
is what you are made bold to say
when facing the legalistic integrity of
John Winthrop—not to mention the
holy wath of Hugh Peters, the satiric
antifeminism of Nathaniel Ward, and
the sheer adamant intolerance of John
Endicott. Behind her last claim—as
Hawthorne well knows—lies a series of
far less drastic attempts to affirm that
the Spirit does not always obey the
laws of ordinary moral appearance.
And even though she has moved from
the dangerous to the intolerable, the
weight of Hawthorne's subtlest moral
judgment falls no more heavily on her
head than on those of her judges.

In simple ironic fact, she is their
natural opposite—induced into individualistic heresy by their organized,
legalistic intolerance in much the same
way as Hester's later denials are induced by the violence of the community's over-response. Beginning, apparently, with only a purer sort of Calvinism than was customarily preached
in New England, Mrs. Hutchinson's ultimate claim to a totally self-sufficient
private illumination seems the inevitable response to an emerging Puritan
orthodoxy which, in its undeniable
tendency to conflate the visible with
the invisible church, was really claiming that for nearly all valid human
purposes the "chosen of men" *were*
the "sealed of heaven." If the com-

munity overextends and mystifies its
authority, the individual will trust the
deepest passional self to nullify it all.
Or at least "the woman" will.

What Hawthorne's figure of Mrs.
Hutchinson suggests is that "the woman" is not by essence the safe and
conserving social force the seventeenth
and the nineteenth century (and much
Hawthorne criticism) decreed her to
be. On the contrary female sexuality
seems, in its concentration and power,
both a source for and a type of individualistic nullification of social restraint.
Obviously Hawthorne's feelings about
this are not without ambivalence.
Personally, of course, he would always
prefer some less powerful, more submissive 'Phoebe"; and in one way or
another he would continue to protest
that "Woman's intellect should never
give the tone to that of man," that her
"morality is not exactly the material
for masculine virtue" (XII, 217-18).
But his clear recognition of the anti-
social meaning of self-conscious female
sexuality, first formulated in the theological context of Puritan heresy, goes
a long way toward explaining the
power and the pathos of Hester Prynne.

Hawthorne reformulates his insight
in "The Gentle Boy." Despite the
complexities introduced by a "calm"
male enthusiast and by the presence
of the "rational piety" of that unreconstructed lover of home and children
named Dorothy Pearson, we can hardly
miss the elemental clash between "the
female," Quaker Catherine, and the
entire legalistic, repressive Puritan establishment. Against that male system
of enforced rationalistic uniformity,
she extravagantly testifies to the
reality of an inspired and pluralistic
freedom. Her response is, of course,
extreme; Hawthorne is no more than
faithful to history in judging it so
(even though he does not have her
walk naked through the streets of

he Puritan capital). But, in a terrify-
ng and elemental way, her response
s effective. Tobias Pearson can only
puzzle over and feel guilty about his
drift toward the sect whose doctrines
he thinks quite irresponsible; but this
"muffled female" *must* stand up in
the midst of a Puritan congregation
(authoritatively and symbolically
divided, by a wide aisle, into male and
female) and denounce the minister's
cruel and sterile formulation of the
Puritan way.

The relevance of Quaker Catherine
for Hester Prynne is simple and evident:
here is the woman who has *not* been
prevented from joining hands with
Ann Hutchinson; her enthusiasm (and
her sufferings) are such that not even
little Ilbrahim can hold her back from
a career of public testimony to the
autonomous authority of conscience
itslef. Quaker Catherine does "come
down to us *in history*, hand in hand
with Ann Hutchinson." No doubt
several historical women lie behind
Hawthorne's figural portrait of Quaker
Catherine, but surely none more
powerfully than Mary Dyer, Ann
Hutchinson's strongest female ally—
who literally took her hand and accompanied her out of Cotton's church
after her excommunication, went with
her into exile, and (years after Mrs.
Hutchinson had been providentially
slaughtered by the Indians) went on
to become notorious in the Quaker
invasion of Massachusetts.

Accordingly, another level of history
is also involved: virtually all commentators have recognized that in New
England, in dialectic with the Puritan
Way, Ann Hutchinson and the Quakers
go together; that the latter represent,
chiefly a more organized and self-
consciously sectarian espousal of the
values of individualistic (or "spiritual")
freedom which is the essence of Ann
Hutchinson's doctrine. If one is com-

mitted and hostile, the cry against
both is simply devilish and seductive
enthusiasm, unregenerate impulse
breaking all bonds of restraint and
decorum. If one is committed and
sympathetic, the cry is just as simple:
the martyrdom of human dignity
and divine freedom by aggressive
repression. If one is a cautious modern
commentator, one can only pity the
victims and worry that both the
Hutchinsonian and the (seventeenth-
century) Quaker doctrines do rather
tend to elevate the "individual conscience above all authority"; that
both promote a "monistic egotism"
which tends to dissolve "all those
psychological distinctions man had
invented to 'check, circumscribe, and
surpass himself.'"

None of these formulations would
have been unfamiliar to Hawthorne.
And neither would his knowledge or
speculation be significantly advanced
by the modern historian who, after
discussing the Ann Hutchinson question as a "Pre-Quaker Movement,"
begins his chapters on Quakerism
proper with the observation that as
in London and at the great Universities
of England, "so too, the first Quakers
to reach the American hemisphere were
women." In every way it comes to
seem the reverse of surprising that
radical freedom and awakened female
sexuality are inextricably linked in
Hawthorne's most obviously historical
romance. History itself had forged the
link.

What is perhaps surprising is that
Hawthorne is as sympathetic to a sex-
related understanding of freedom as
he is. His "Mrs. Hutchinson" is a profoundly troubled and dangerous woman; his Quaker Catherine becomes,
in her "unbridled fanaticism," guilty
of violating her most sacred duties
(even if Ilbrahim is *not* a Christ-figure);
even his Hester Prynne is far from the

"Saint" she has occasionally been made out to be. But Hawthorne sympathizes with the problems as deeply as he fears the dangers; his compulsion to record warnings is no stronger than his desire to discover the laws by which powerful half truths generate their opposites or to feel the pain of those being destroyed by that implacable dialectic.

• • •

We are now, finally, in a position to "begin"—to look directly at Hester walking in the footsteps of Ann Hutchinson, and to approach *The Scarlet Letter* itself in the one historical context Hawthorne seems most urgently to suggest.

• • •

The experiences of Hester and Dimmesdale are subject to an exquisite (and painful) historical conditioning. Their Puritan world may be, as in another formulation, some version of the "modern" world, but this is far too imprecise to account for the historical specificity of Hawthorne's intention and achievement. To be sure, *The Scarlet Letter* details the items of Hester's beliefs even less than the early sketch specifies those of Mrs. Hutchinson; and yet the romance undoubtedly is, as one very excellent reading describes it, a "literary exercise in moral theology." That theology is, so far as the *characters* are concerned, "Puritan." So profoundly Puritan are the historically conditioned experiences of Hester and Dimmesdale, in fact, that *The Scarlet Letter* must be seen as Hawthorne's way of testing the limits of Puritan theology as a way of making sense out of the deepest and most passionate human experience. The limits of that theology are understood by Hawthorne to be—what I take it in fact they are—antinomian; and those antinomian limits of Puritan theology are

associated by Hawthorne—as they were by his orthodox predecessors—with "the woman." When the limits are reached, as historically they were and as philosophically they must be, the theology fails what a twentieth-century critic of Puritanism has called "the pragmatic test." And as the theology fails, *The Scarlet Letter* becomes (in the context of the Ann Hutchinson problem, at least) a powerful contribution to what a nineteenth-century critic called "the moral argument against Calvinism."

The Scarlet Letter is about the reasons why "the woman" Hester Prynne reaches certain antinomian conclusions not unlike those of Ann Hutchinson; and why, though her progress seems somehow necessary, and though personally she enlists our deepest sympathies, both the tale and the teller force her to abandon those conclusions. More elliptically, it is also about Dimmesdale's lesser portion of the "strange fire"; about the failure of his Cottonesque, semi-antinomian theology; and, in the end, about his much-misunderstood "neonomian" emphasis on "the law" and "the sin." If we understand Hawthorne's relation to Mather, Johnson, and Winthrop properly, we can profitably view *The Scarlet Letter* as Hawthrone's own *Short Story of the Rise, Reign and Ruine of the Antinomians, Familists, and Libertines.*

In these terms, Hester's career is fairly easy to plot. At the outset she is not unambiguously antinomian. But she is conceived, like Hawthorne's Ann Hutchinson, as a woman who bears "trouble in her own bosom" (XII, 219); and her "desperate recklessness" on the scaffold, symbolized by the flagrancy of her embroidered "A." and issuing in "a haughty smile, and a glance that would not be abashed" (52), seems deliberately to recall Mrs.

Hutchinson's courtroom defiance:

She stands loftily before her judges with a determined brow; and, unknown to herself, there is a flash of carnal pride half hidden in her eye, as she surveys the many learned and famous men whom her doctrines have put in fear. (XII, 224)

That might describe Hester easily enough. She begins, let us say, in a not very repentant spirit. Strong hints of her later denials and unorthodox affirmations are already there.

To be sure, Hester feels a deep sense of shame, and we scarcely need the still, small quasi-authorial voice of a young-woman spectator to tell us so; the "reduction" of Ann Hutchinson's doctrinal bastard to a living illegitimate child must, in a Puritan community, at least, count for something. And yet even here Hester feels little enough of what we should call "guilt." Just after the trauma of public exposure, she does confess a real wrong done to Chillingworth; but defiance of hopelessly unqualified and painfully uncomprehending male judges seems clearly the dominant element in her early characterization. It is probably true to say that (ignoring the "epilogue") Hester is nearer to "repentance" at the very opening of *The Scarlet Letter* than she ever is again. But she is not very near it. And by the time she finds herself in the forest with Dimmesdale, she has evidently found that she "should never have cause to be sorry for sinne" again.

For that antinomian moment, the narrator severely instructs us, Hesters "whole seven years of outlaw and ignominy had been little other than a preparation" (200). The moment includes not only the decision to cast by all outward pretense of living by the Puritan "world's law" and run away

with Dimmesdale but also, and even more radically, her attempt to convince that unreconstructed Puritan theologian that what they earlier did "had a consecration of its own"—they having felt it so and said so to each other. The painfulness of Hester's development toward this moment in no way lessens our sense of its inevitability. From the first she has seemed perilously close to defying her judges with the affirmation that her spirit posits and obeys its own law.

• • •

Her own version of the antinomian heresy does not, obviously, express itself in theological jargon; for the most part Hawthorne eschewed it even in treating Mrs. Hutchinson. No dogmatist, Hawthorne is looking for differences that *make* a difference; and the antinomian difference is identically expressed in Mrs. Hutchinson and Hester Prynne, in association with but not quite reduced to a discovery and affirmation of the legitimacy of their female sexuality. Call it Spirit with the seventeenth, or Passional Self with a later century, one's affirmation is not very different: the significance of a life is *not* the sum of its legally regulated outward works; or, more radically, what one does has a consecration of its own provided the quality of deep inner feeling is right—i.e., authentic.

Now plainly this is all too partial a truth for Hawthorne; we are not wrong in hearing his own advice when Dimmesdale twice bids Hester's revolutionary voice to "Hush." And yet he understands how it all comes about. He even presents it as necessary for Hester to reach this stage of self-affirmation and release from shame before she can settle into anything approaching final peace.

• • •

Waiving the problem of vehicle and

tenor, we may validly conclude that in *The Scarlet Letter* "the woman's discovery of an authentic, valid, and not shameful sexual nature is not unlike the Self's discovery of its own interior, "spiritual" sanction. The *donnée* of Hawthorne's romance is such that Hester discovers both together, and each reinforces the other.

And further, by way of completing our contextual approach to *The Scarlet Letter*, it seems appropriate to suggest that Hawthorne's treatment of Dimmesdale, the less clearly antinomian partner, provides cogent reasons for not divorcing the theology from, or reducing it too simply to, the sexuality. For Dimmesdale's predicament is not to be understood without some fairly explicit reference to the most theological of the antinomian questions—certainly not without a sense of the peculiar moral shapes one can be molded into only by a fairly high Calvinism. Indeed there is, as I have already suggested, strong evidence that Hawthorne thought of Dimmesdale as some intellectual and literary relative of John Cotton.

In a number of related senses, Dimmesdale's problem is "hypocrisy." Most simply, he is not what he outwardly appears; he may or may not be "vile," but he is not the apotheosis of saintly purity the Puritan community takes him for. More technically, he is an enforcing agent of public discipline who has himself sinned against a clear and serious public law whose absolute validity he (unlike Hester) never questions for a moment; and who refuses to confess and submit to the discipline he has sworn by covenant to uphold and enforce. In so refusing, he may very well be avoiding the question of whether he is really sorry for his sin, or whether in fact he loves his own satisfactions more than he loves God;

if so, if Dimmesdale's adultery is really "idolatry," as in the common religious equivalence, then of course he is a "hypocrite" in the very most technical Puritan sense of all: he is an unconverted man who has found his way not only *in to* but to the very *apex* of the purest church the world has ever known. This is clearly what he fears: that the minister, whose election is sure if anyone's is, whose conversion is the norm for the members' admission, and who—at this level, incidentally—is universally revered as a miracle of preternatural holiness and supernatural humility, is really an unregenerate sinner simply.

He fears, but he is not certain. He also hopes. In such tension Dimmesdale is a classic Puritan case of conscience—an advanced and exacerbated form of the too-common problem of lingering sinfulness and naturally attendant doubt which seems to have followed most honest Puritans into full communion with New England's congregations of "visible saints." What, after all, could the unreconstructed Arminianism of natural conscience make of the fact that after one professed to have received saving grace by the direct operation of the spirit (and had that profession accepted by all other spiritual men) one continued to be roughly the same sort of moral person one was before?

The simple answer is antinomianism: "works" argue nothing. The sons of God being under no law, it is as fatal a confusion to argue from the presence of sin to the absence of grace as it is to infer justification of the person from sanctification of the life. Grace is a spiritual indwelling, and whatever the Spirit is, is right. Just ask Hester.

Dimmesdale, of course, can accept this limit-interpretation of Pauline and Protestant theology as little as Cotton could. And yet Dimmesdale seems caught in a trap set for him by certain of the spiritual principles Cotton laid down carefully to distinguish himself from both the covenant legalists on the one side and the "antinomians, familists, and libertines" on the other. Everyone wanted to admit that the forensic transaction of justification did not imply or create immediate and perfect operational sanctity, but Cotton's critics wanted him to narrow the gap as much as Protestant loyalty could possibly admit. They put it to him: when you say "A Christian may have assurance of his good estate maintained to him when the frame of his Spirit and course is grown much degenerate, we want much satisfaction." Your doctrine is very dangerous, they instructed him; there ought to be more "symmetry and proportion" in this matter of "faith and holiness" or you "open a wide door of temptation, as into Sin with less fear, so into a bold continuance and slight healing of sin, and breaches thereby."

As always, the legalists have conceived the problem rather too crudely: Dimmesdale's "continuance," for example, is far from "bold," and his physical and moral self-flagellations amount at some level to more than a "slight healing of sin." And yet there is sense in their position. A man who *fears* he may be a hypocrite and yet has good theological reasons to *hope* that even gross sins do not necessarily prove the case either way is likely to clutch at every available theological straw. And indeed Cotton's answer to the legalists offers far more than a straw. It is worth quoting at some length for it marvellously illuminates Dimmesdale's predicament. If a man

> know the riches of Gods grace in Christ,
> he ordinarily both may, and (by ordinary
> rule) ought to believe that his justified
> estate doth still remain unshaken, not

withstanding his grievous sin. For as Justification and the faith of it doth not stand upon his good works, so neither doth it fall or fail upon his evil work.

Cotton's difference from the antinomians is, evidently, a fairly subtle one—and not of primary interest to us here. Of significance is the fact that the strictest Calvinist of New England's first generation provides Dimmesdale with a perfectly plausible way to avoid the obvious, most "natural" conclusion about his technical hypocrisy.

And Cotton brings the case even closer to our own:

> Because men of great measure of holiness be apt to live besides their faith, in the strength of their own gifts and not in the strength of Christ, it pleaseth the Lord sometimes to leave them to greater falls, than other weaker Christians, who being of weaker gifts do find more need to live by faith in Christ than upon the strength of their gifts.

It seems to me entirely likely that some conception such as this—a highly religious man being tested by a great fall —lies very close to Hawthorne's idea of Dimmesdale. And that Hawthorne is testing this Cottonesque way of conceptualizing the problem of sin and sainthood as he watches Dimmesdale fail to work out his salvation in these terms.

For the terms do fail him, even more plainly than, in the epilogue, Hester's appear to have failed her. The phycological dynamic of their failure is delicately wrought, but it is "there," in the romance. To see it requires only to look at Dimmesdale's few key speeches very closely.

We do not begin to get inside Dimmesdale until Chapter X, where "The Leech" is working on "His Patient." With the worst imaginable motives,

Chillingworth is trying to get Dimmesdale to do what the structure and basic conception of the romance clearly indicates he must if he is to save his soul, in any imaginable sense—clearly and openly admit his guilt, whatever the consequences. Dimmesdale offers several "good" reasons why some men find it impossible to confess before the Last Day, or to any but the Searcher of Hearts. His reasons are all, we easily sense, speculative or notional, unreal; the two men are talking "objectively" about "some men." And yet before Dimmesdale waives the whole subject as if "irrelevant or unreasonable," he is betrayed into a modestly revealing hint. The best of his rationalizations is that "some men" do not confess because in spite of their sin they yet retain "a zeal for God's glory and man's welfare"; they realize that once exposed "no good can be achieved by them; no evil of the past be redeemed by better service" (132). Hypocrisy, Dimmesdale seems to argue, is not without an important social, even spiritual use.

• • •

The irony here is very keen. It seems impossible to escape the sense that Hawthorne is deliberately playing with one of the most famous arguments in a massive Puritan literature of propagandistic self-defense—the idea of "the usefulness of hypocrites." Attacked by English Presbyterians for a wildly utopian collapse of the invisible church into the visible, defenders of the New England Way loudly protested that they fully *expected* to receive hypocrites into their churches, despite the revolutionary tests for saving grace; that they indeed could rest easy in this practical knowledge, despite their purist theoretic aims, because in outward practice the hypocrite was very often more zealous, set a more striking public example

than the true saint. The most authoritative spokesman for this Puritan "foreign policy" was—of course—John Cotton.

The irony is only slightly less telling when we remember that neither Dimmesdale nor Hawthorne really sees the case in these terms. Hawthorne could very *easily* accept hypocrites into *his* church, since it is universal and consists *only* of hypocrites who never *can* fully "show forth" what they ultimately are. Limited to his historic world, however, Dimmesdale is obviously far from this insight. Indeed he is even farther away from it than his use-of-hypocrites rationalization would indicate.

Where he is, morally and theologically speaking, becomes perfectly clear only in the forest with Hester—though anyone versed in the literary cure of Puritan souls senses it long before. The meaning of his entire predicament is encapsulated into two sentences, and logically enough he speaks them in direct reply to Hester's antinomian plan for adulterous escape:

> "If, in all these past seven years," thought he, "I could recall one instant of peace or hope, I would yet endure, for the sake of that earnest of Heaven's mercy. But now, —since I am irrevocably doomed,—wherefore should I not snatch the solace allowed to the condemned culprit before his execution?" (201)

Again the irony is fairly complex. First of all we recognize in Dimmesdale's decision to "seize the day" the crassest sort of antinomian response possible for a Calvinist to make: since I am predestined to hell anyway, I might as well. . . . But this is the least of it. More crucially, Dimmesdale reveals that he has to this point been looking at his life in a way that is very "properly" Calvinist: he has been regarding his acts, good and evil, and his spiritual states, hopeful and discouraging, not as sequential parts of a moral life that is *building*, bit by bit, but rather as *evidences* of his status relative to divine decree. The difference may often seem subtle in practice, but it is absolutely profound; and the meaning is to be read in any Puritan diary. One does not repent sin in order to undo it and atone for it and get back into divine favor; only Catholics and other Arminians think this. Rather one examines sins along with every other significant fact about the moral life in order to detect, if one possibly can, whether or not an eternal decree of salvation has made itself temporally manifest as a spiritual experience of justification, usually issuing more or less "proportionally and symmetrically" in sanctification.

For *most* Puritans sins are, therefore, an essential sign; for *all*, repentance is an absolutely necessary one. Even for Cotton. The great man may have great sins and not lose heart and hope; but even the great man must find that he truly *can* repent. Gross outward lapses may be at best a crude indicator of the spiritual estate, but enduring love of sin is not.

"Of penance," Dimmesdale admits—of that melodramatic outward punishment and gothic inward torture—there has been a surfeit; "Of penitence," however—of that true spiritual rejection of the soul's rejection of God—"there has been none!" (192). And now, he concludes, things look very bad indeed. He may as well admit he has been, all along, the hypocrite he feared he might be and yet hoped (in spite of his rationalization to Chillingworth) he might not be. In the forest then, finally, after seven years of self-torturing hope against hope, Dimmesdale gives over the attempt to see himself as the man whose justification does

not, in Cotton's words, "Fall or fail upon his evil works." Semi-antinomian to this point, he now concludes that his hope has all been in vain—that he has not repented his sin, that he has been granted no further spiritual assurances, and that his crime of adultery is precisely what all vulgar Puritanism would take it to be, "visible" (if only to himself) evidence of manifest unregeneracy.

Spiritually, then, Dimmesdale is further from Hester Prynne during their sexual reunion in the forest than he has ever been before—as far away, in fact, as it is possible to be within a Puritan world. Their decision to escape, though they may "say it" to each other, means two dramatically opposed things. To Hester it is that triumphant escape into the higher antinomian freedom of spiritual self-reliance; to Dimmesdale it is a pitiful retreat from the hope-against-hope to that miserable alternative of sinful freedom left to the despairing reprobate. One may wish their original adulterous meeting involved more of real mutuality.

Thus Hawthorne's subtlest view of Dimmesdale is as a man who is so ineffectual an antinomian as not to be able to overcome the conscientious suspicion that his serious sin proves him a hypocrite; not even with the subtle categories of John Cotton. Hawthorne's men, as we know, are weaker than his women. Or perhaps it is simply that "woman's morality is not quite the standard for masculine virtue." Or perhaps he is simply honest. In any event, neither his sexuality nor his doctrine can justify the life he has been leading or, now, sanctify the new freedom he has been seduced into accepting. He will run away, in a sense, to settle his doubts, once and for all, into a certainty of reprobation.

• • •

At the last moment, of course, a

major reversal occurs. Ceasing to "live in the strength of [his] own gifts"— even though he has just exercised them magnificently in a bad-faith election sermon—Dimmesdale asks for Hester's strength and God's grace to help him up the scaffold. Once there, his words indicate that somehow he has freed himself from his old Calvinist entrapment. If he has not entirely de-theologized himself, at least he has got his doctrine down to certain saving essentials. Hester calls on his far-seeing vision to predict their final destiny. But Dimmesdale, who has been reading evidences of *faits accomplis* for too long, rightly refuses to predict: "Hush, Hester, hush!" What has often been called his final "gloom" is no more than elemental moral and theological honesty. "The law we broke!—the sin here so awfully revealed!" Stern instructions to an Antinomian. Yet these alone must be in their thoughts, their only proper concern. For the rest, "God knows; and He is merciful!" (256).

Law, Sin, Mercy—these are now the only terms in Dimmesdale's new moral scheme. We know there are laws to restrict our Selves in the name of our communities which, well or ill, sustain our common life; we know we break these laws; the rest is up to God. This may or may not conceal Arminian heresy, but "neo-nomian" Hawthorne has clearly designed it to be. I think we may grant the writer of "Young Goodman Brown" and "The Minister's Black Veil," and the creator of Dimmesdale's problems of ever "outering" what he truly is inside, the right to affirm the operational primacy of "the public."

It takes Hester longer, and it requires a years-later epilogue, but she too relents from her doctrine of the autonomous private—she repents, turns her game of "penance" into authentic "penitence." She still holds out for a feminist reformer, but she can now separate the valid sexual expectations of her sisterhood from the supposed spiritual freedom of the Self from the world's law.

The final ironies of Hawthorne's use of Hutchinsonian motifs and antinomian ideas are striking indeed. If his early sketch seems to reduce a dangerous female heretic to a sexual case, his effort can be regarded as a commentary on a Puritan response as validly as it can be taken for his own; and, he puts *all* the subtlety back into *The Scarlet Letter*. He maintains, even literalizes, all the sexual suggestions in his creation of Hester Prynne, but he leaves them in tension with some very profound (if, for him, dangerous) religious ideas. With Dimmesdale he allows the full theological complexity to operate, though we never forget that Dimmesdale is related to Hester in the sexual problems which form the context of their spiritual struggles. The perfect context, we feel, given Puritan problems with "privacy" of all sorts. And in the end, after he has fully explored the antinomian and Cottonesque ramifications of his imaginative vision of a Puritan heresy, in doctrine and in metaphoric implication, Hawthorne brings both his principal characters back to something like his own "neo-nomian" norm. The ending is by no means "happy"—any more than Hawthorne's "Antinomians" and "Libertines" are in any sense that would satisfy Winthrop or Mather "Ruined." But their "Short Story" does end in an important doctrinal transformation.

The Self is not to be regularly inferred from its Works; it is quite naive to think so. But human sin, guilt, and sorrow are not to be transcended or "spiritually" suspended in this life. The Self is spiritually more free than any human establishment, theocratic or otherwise, can recognize or "tolerate." But the world's law validly exists to restrain our disruptive social excesses, however powerful and authentic we feel or "say" their private consecration to be. That, or something like it, equally simple, was the usable historical truth to be discovered from a tracing of Ann Hutchinson's footsteps.

Many of the supporters of Anne Hutchinson ended their lives as Quakers. The similarities between the views of the Massachusetts sectary and those of the Quaker leader George Fox are many. The role which women such as Anne Hutchinson sought in the Puritan Congregational churches was denied them; women in the Society of Friends, the Quakers, were allowed a share in governance and a role in defining doctrine. In this article Mary Maples Dunn investigates the reasons for the failure of Congregational women and the success of Quaker women. She offers an explanation of Anne Hutchinson's failure and helps to place the role of women in early America in proper perspective.

MARY MAPLES DUNN

"Saints and Sisters"

It is frequently observed in Christian societies that the women go to church. The implication is that the church, or even religion, is in some way more necessary to women than to men, although women are submissive to the men who dominate the priesthoods. But how and why this gender differentiation develops in respect to religion is imperfectly understood; we are not certain that it is inherent in Christianity itself; we do not know why it becomes part of a social-religious order, what functions it might have in that society, nor what conditions produce the dichotomy. American experience in the seventeenth and early eighteenth centuries offers the historian two Protestant cases to investigate and contrast, the Puritan Congregationalists and the Quakers. Puritans and Quakers pursued different routes to settlement in America, with different results for women.

The religious intensity and excitement in England prior to and during the Civil War gave rise to both Puritanism and Quakerism, and provided a background in which a rethinking of

Christian doctrine was taking place and church governance and church-state relationships were being questioned. This fluid situation was particularly important to women. The Protestant dismissal of the cult of Mary and of the nunneries opened up questions about the position of women, both in society and in the structure of the church, and destroyed the most powerful female religious symbol and role model. The result was a period of intense religious activity in which Puritan and Quaker women in America took part. Indeed, removal to America may have been particularly invigorating to the Protestant women who took part in these religious migrations, because of the sense shared by both men and women that they were free from traditional restraints. But in Puritan Congregationalism, despite the vigor and enthusiasm of the first generation women, women were disciplined to accept male authority, socialized to submission, and accustomed to filling the churches. Amongst Quakers we discover religious experience and church governance more equally shared by women and men.

There were at least three factors that determined these different outcomes for women in the "City on a Hill" and the "Holy Experiment." First, it was necessary to the development of a predominantly female piety that there be some objectives of the society that required female piety, and at least to some extent excused it in men. Second, scripture had to be interpreted in a way that asserted female inferiority. Therefore, the interests of those who had the power to formulate doctrine and interpret the word of God were determinants of the female role. The third factor is related to the second. Those who had the power to exert discipline over women

had power to socialize them in the church.

The Puritan development precedes the Quaker one. The first generation of Puritan immigrants to America were not yet sectarians; they were groping their way toward a form of church governance which would be free from the evils of episcopacy. The godly, both inside and outside the ministry, were making their way toward a doctrinal position that would explain their sense of communion with God. The lines between lay and clerical authority were blurred. Puritans certainly brought in their baggage a sense of the inferiority of women; but belief in female equality before the Lord also made it uncertain what role women would play in a new religious order.

The fundamental statement of female inferiority was, of course, found in Genesis. Eve, the first to listen to Satan and the seducer of Adam, brought to women a heavy share of original sin; and to Adam, to man, the message that he should have known better than to listen to woman. Woman in this case was also a vehicle for Satan, not able to see through his wiles, wanting in intellect, needing protection. Genesis 3:16 imposed the correction and punishment: "Unto the woman he said, I will greatly increase thy sorrow, & thy conceptions. In sorrow shalt thou bring forth children, and thy desire shall be subject to thine husband, and he shall rule over thee." The Calvinist sense of original sin was powerful, and it was unlikely that Puritans could ever reject the notion that God required submission of women.

The traditional Christian rules which might govern the place and conduct of a woman in the church, and the authorities she should seek in matters of doctrine, were asserted for Puritans by St. Paul. Paul was widely accepted as authority by those who wished to recapitulate in their own time the primitive Christian church, and he was therefore important to New World Puritans. Paul seemed to make his position clear in his letters to the Corinthians and, later, to Timothy and Titus. In I Cor. 14:34-35 he said, "Let your women keep silence in the Churches: for it is not permitted unto them to speak: but they ought to be subject, as also the Law saith. And if they will learn any thing, let them ask their husbands at home: for it is a shame for a woman to speak in the Church." It was not possible to construe this injunction narrowly as to time and place, that is, only to Corinth, since the Apostle was equally specific in the later letter to Timothy (1 Tim. 2:11-12), "Let the women learn in silence with all subjection. I permit not a woman to teach, neither to usurp authority over the man, but to be in silence."

Paul apparently derived these rules from the customs with which he was familiar; he may have asserted them at first only for Corinth, and later re-affirmed them in the realization that the end of human time was not, after all, at hand. This could account for the fact that in other ways Paul had a more liberating message for women. In Titus 2:3-4, older women were given a teaching function: "teachers of honest things, they may instruct the young women to be sober minded, that they love their husbands, that they love their children." Paul also insisted that women were to share equally in the benefits of the new order. He wrote to the Galatians (3:28), "There is neither Jew nor Grecian: there is neither bond nor free: there is neither male nor female: for you are all one in Christ Jesus." Furthermore, even in the first letter to the Corinthians

there is some confusion, since he said in 1 Cor. 11:3-5, "But I will that you know, that Christ is the head of every man: & the man is the woman's head: and God is Christ's head. Every man praying or prophecying having any thing on his head, dishonoreth his head. But every woman that prayeth or prophecieth bareheaded, dishonoreth her head: for it is even one very thing, as though she were shaven." The implication of inferiority is clear; but so is the possibility of speaking in the church, and the ancient Biblical tradition of women prophets receives recognition.

The people of New England could, if they wanted, find in Paul a situation parallel to their own: a radical spiritual message of equality in tension with social custom. It was not certain how the tension between these two views of women would be resolved in New England, and in this situation (which may have obtained at all times and on all frontiers in the Christian religion) many women engaged themselves in both experiments in church governance and in the discussion of doctrine. A few of them made their marks.

Women shared fully in the excitement that creation of a new religious settlement produced, and they responded to the challenge with intelligence, vigor, and enthusiasm. The covenanted or gathered church was a source of a feeling of equality. Women also tried to control doctrines in many areas, including those relating specifically to women. Unfortunately, heresy trials constitute much of the evidence that women tried to assert themselves. This is unfortunate because those charged with heresy were considered extremists whom the Puritans rejected and because these women were more apt to perish than to publish. Their trial records are our only evidence of their doctrinal positions, and those

records were written by male opponents. Nevertheless, they are ample
testimony that women were neither
silent nor submissive.

Anne Hutchinson is the most famous of these women, because the
doctrine that she, John Cotton, and
their followers tried to bring to general acceptance in Boston would have
changed profoundly the thrust of the
Massachusetts experiment. Hutchinson and the Antinomians rejected the
doctrine of sanctification or the "Covenant of Works" (the idea that outward behavior or a righteous life was
a sign of justification or redemption
of one's soul by Christ). Their own
doctrine, or "Covenant of Grace,"
insisted that redemption came only
through the gift of grace. Hutchinson's own knowledge of this was
her sense of direct communion with
the Holy Spirit. In the Antinomian
view, the Covenant of Works had a
deadening effect on the spiritual life
of the community because it encouraged too much scrutiny of behavior
and led to formalism or legalism in
establishing rules of behavior which,
consistently observed, would prepare
for or offer evidence of election by
God to sainthood. The Antinomians
acquired a following that threatened
a breakdown in Massachusetts' ideological unity, an overturning of the
authority of law and therefore of
social discipline, and a real revolution
in the norms for Christian (Puritan)
behavior. It was possible for a woman
to share in the leadership of such a
movement because the Covenant of
Grace could free her from restraints
emanating from a rigid application of
the rules of a Covenant of Works.

The story of Hutchinson's trial
and defeat is too well known to need
retelling here. However, it is worth
pointing out again that she was a
tough woman, intelligent and learned,

determined to remake the church. She
had remarkable vigor and a charisma
that might have changed the course of
Massachusetts history had she been a
man. It was clear that her judges,
particularly John Winthrop, thought
she headed a "potent party" and was
a formidable enemy. They were determined to get rid of her. She was a good
match for them in all theological dis-
cussions, and over and over again in
the trial they were forced to revert to
the issue of women speaking and
teaching. Hutchinson insisted that she
worked within the Pauline rules; her
judges were sure she did not.

At the heart of their disagreement
was the fact that Hutchinson applied
Paul in a positive way to her situation,
while her judges were determined to
stick to the reading most restricting
for women. For example, she maintained that in the large meetings held
in her house to discuss sermons, she
could speak because this was private,
that is, not in the church; that she
could, as an older woman, teach
younger women; that she could, when
asked, teach and counsel men in private.
But she also declared a right to public
utterance in exercising a gift of
prophesy, for which she found Biblical
precedent. Her judges decided that
the age of prophesy was over. Finally,
". . . to justify this her disordered
course, she said she walked by the rule
of the Apostle, Gal. which she called
the rule of the new creature . . . ."
[italics added], that is, Gal. 3:28
"there is neigher male nor female: for
you are all one in Christ Jesus." Hutchinson insisted, then, in applying the
broadest possible definition of Christian responsibility to women's roles in
religion. Because she argued in the
context of a situation which seemed
to her judges to be threatening to the
Puritan establishment, they were not
able to consider the problem dispas-

sionately, and the judgment against her was the most important decision Puritans made about women's place in the formulation of doctrine.

Aggressive women were also evident in conservative New Haven seven years after Hutchinson's defeat, which had influenced attitudes toward women everywhere in the Puritan settlements. In 1644 a heretic woman of high status disturbed the peace of New Haven. Anne Eaton, daughter of an English bishop and the unhappy wife of Theophilus Eaton, the governor, was tried and excommunicated. Her fall from grace first arose from her disavowal of infant baptism; she had been led to error by reading and failure to seek guidance from her husband. Because she was the wife of the governor, her example was considered important to the development of the community. When the governor's wife walked out of church, there was hell to pay. Minister, elders, and husband were quick to go to work to convince her of the error of her ways. She was steadily hounded, particularly by the minister, John Davenport, who had played a small role in the trial of Anne Hutchinson.

Anne Eaton either could not or would not argue her own case, and while she refused to accept the authority of her male opponents in a matter of doctrine, the trial record does not give any evidence that she argued for her own ability to make decisions. But heresy on the question of infant baptism was not the only ground on which the church moved against her. In the end, Eaton was excommunicated for lying and stubbornness (that is, for refusal to discuss the matter) and censured on additional charges which sprang from bad relations with other members of her household: her mother-in-law, her grown stepdaughter, and several servants. It would appear that by

1644 intellectual error alone would not serve as grounds to proceed against a woman because, strictly speaking, heresy was beyond her capacity. Women had lost the battle for control over doctrine, which now belonged to men.

• • •

The cases of Eaton and Hutchinson are both tied into social and political factors that overwhelmed the women, increased the bias of their judges, and prejudiced their communities. The question whether women may have played a more active "mainstream" role in religion and church governance is difficult to answer; women who achieved small-scale successes didn't so readily break into the records.

However, some evidence of aggressive females and a church seemingly more open to the formulation of less limiting policies for women is found in the notebook or diary of John Fiske (1637-1675), a clergyman of Wenham. In this church, in which the pastor always referred to his congregation as "the brethren and sisters," and usually fully identified women (that is, he used both the father's and husband's names and the woman's Christian name), there was brisk debate in the 1640s over female membership. It was argued first that women themselves had publicly to relate their religious experiences and their sense of election, if the church were to judge their fitness for membership. Therefore the act of qualification seemed to require women to speak in church. The diary noted that in some churches men, elders or ministers, were reading the women's statements, on the grounds that women should keep silent; and Wenham produced scriptural examples of female prophets to justify female public speaking of this kind. The case was similar to the one made by Anne Hutchinson.

Secondly, Wenham church decided

that women were not automatically transferred from one church to another when their husbands moved, and it badgered the Salem church to get individual dismissions for women. The issue appears to have been pushed by one Joan White, who also took an active role in church governance; she spoke in church meetings and made motions which the congregation acted upon. In her relation, she said that she "was brought up in a poore Ignorand place," and although she came to New England because she believed good people came there, she was "for a long space of time living far in ye woods, from the means; and reading on Rom 10, Faith commeth by hearing; put her affections onward ye desire of ye means." In short, she wanted to get out of the woods and into a church, and was enjoying every minute of it. . . .

Wenham church gives us a number of aggressive women, behaving independently, taking an active role in church governance, and being taken seriously. Then in late 1655, Fiske and a number of his followers moved from Wenham to Chelmsford, where they started a new church. In establishing local practices, they concluded in early 1656, "this day agrrd [sic] by ye church yt ye officer should repeate & declare ye Relation of ye wo: to ye church." In the following decade fewer and fewer women appear in Fiske's pages, and in Chelmsford as in almost all churches, women were referred to as "wife of"; first names generally went unrecorded. Women lost not only voice, but also identity. Furthermore, the experience in Chelmsford was not unique. By 1660, in all of the church records examined for this study, silence had been enjoined on women in the matter of the relation. Silence also prevented them from having a voice in cases of discipline. Judgment was in

the hands of men, and more and more the minister instructed the brethren in their voting. Women seem to have been disciplined in numbers out of proportion to their share of congregational populations, and their offenses were increasingly connected with social behavior, not with heresy. What had happened?

Certainly women continued to respond positively to the church, far more so than the men. Scattered admissions data for 28 Congregational churches (18 from Massachusetts and 10 from Connecticut) show a steady growth in the proportion of female admissions. In the 1630s and 1640s male and female admissions were fairly equal, but a shift began in the 1650s, and after 1660 female admissions exceed male. This numerical superiority holds both in rural and urban areas and throughout the period investigated.

Before 1660 women probably joined the church in numbers somewhat out of proportion to their part of the total population. However, by 1640 women may have accounted for as much as 40 percent of the population, and by 1610, at least in Massachusetts, the sex ratio would have narrowed still further. In any case, the more important point to be developed is women's preponderance in the church population, even after their attempts to share in governance were defeated and male membership shrank.

The best explanation for this phenomenon may come from the anthropologists, who have suggested that all societies tend to esteem male roles more than female ones; and that there is a universal tendency to make what the man does a matter of public importance, what the woman does a domestic matter, carrying less status. New England allows us to add another dimension to these statements: when a society as a whole suffers from a serious conflict in its goals, it can *use* gender role differences to resolve that conflict. It can do this by assigning one set of goals to men, and another to women. This guarantees that those goals which are feminine will become domestic issues and command less social importance. The men can ignore them and apply themselves to male goals.

• • •

The Puritans had not been long in New England before the ministry began to murmur about some decline in piety. When it became clear that they would not be called home to England in triumph, men turned to building a permanent civil society. Historians have long tried both to explain the Puritans' loss of a sense of mission and to discover how they handled their guilt. But it is possible that what was seen as a "declension" was only a loss of *male* piety, that Puritans adopted more stringent gender role differences, and turned their church into a feminine institution. In this church, passive females, ruled over by ministers, would personify Christian virtue. One stage in defusing goal conflict, then, was female dominance in number in the church; it is well known that such organizations lose value when they lose male members.

A number of issues are important in understanding the religious terms of the decline in male admissions. Some ministers understood (where historians have failed) that there were still many *people* joining the church; the problem was that there were fewer men. But they did not seem to comprehend that policies which they and the elders espoused would have the effect of discouraging male admissions. This was because their thrust in church governance was to reduce the role

played by lay men, just as the role of women had been reduced.

• • •

By the turn of the century ministerial rhetoric had validated this symbolic reduction of a Christian congregation to a company of women. Membership was increasingly referred to in terms of the old metaphor of a mystical marriage with Christ. Two funeral sermons illustrate the new emphasis. James Fitch, enumerating the virtues of Anne Mason in 1672, first described her constant attempts to improve her communion with God, in which both "Public Ordinances" and secret prayer and religious conversation played a part. The Lord "gifted her with a measure of Knowledge above what is usual in that Sex" and enabled her to help the afflicted in spirit. She was noted for her works of mercy and made a good death. Thus in 1672 a woman could still be commended for an intellectual and personal approach to religion and salvation, in which introspection and privacy were as important as public acts of faith. There is little to distinguish this from the virtues ascribed to men.

• • •

Women after 1660 could find great reinforcement in religion for the female image most of them had always accepted, and which coincided with their traditional place in the family. To be a good woman was to be a good Christian. But to be a good man was to be a good citizen, active, competitive, self-confident. The women were given, and accepted, the task of preservation of as many values of the Christian community as could be discovered in the family. Only for women did religion and social goals maintain a close correlation. Puritan women, then, subscribed to a Christian role developed out of male needs to pursue social goals no longer validated by religion, out of ministerial determination to control doctrine and governance. They accepted it because of the defeat and discipline of female dissenters, because of the correlation between female socialization into family roles and their place in the church. Perhaps a new role was created, too: as members of the church, women became the keepers of the covenant and protectors of the idea of mission. Put historically, women accepted the burdens of the past, and men the burdens of the future. Put politically, gender differentiation could in this way be seen as a stage in the separation of church and state.

Quaker women were not so bound by either scripture or society as Puritan women. When Pennsylvania was founded in 1682, and Quakers found themselves in control of an important settlement, the sect had already come through its experimental stage and had resolved most major questions of doctrine and of church governance as they applied to women. Quakers were persecuted before 1682, but not directly because of the role women played in the group. Policies in respect to women never threatened the society as a whole, and women had the support of the leaders of the Quaker movement. Both George Fox and Margaret Fell championed female equality and ministries and the inclusion of women in the governance of the Society. William Penn was committed to a policy of religious toleration, and religious unity was never a goal, even in Pennsylvania, as it had been in Massachusetts at the time of the Antinomian crisis. Moreover, Quakers early began to accept their identity as a "peculiar" people who marked themselves as social deviants by such characteristics as their speech,

"hat honor" principle, and refusal to take oaths.

Quakers, in common with other radical sects of seventeenth-century England, but unlike New England Puritans after the Antinomian crisis, believed in spiritual rebirth, direct inspiration by the Divine Light, and lay ministries. All three of these doctrinal positions were important to women. Friends insisted on the possibility of being reborn in the spirit, and on an informing, indwelling Divine Light. Sex bias had no place in this conversion experience; there .was nothing inherent in the female to prevent her spiritual rebirth, to hinder the work of the Divine Light. As Fox put it, in an interesting variation of Paul's message to the Galatians, "Ye are all one *man* in Christ Jesus [italics added] ."

• • •

The first and most notable way in which Quaker women acted upon their dispensation and through the spirit within was to engage in the lay ministry; through this ministry, they could influence doctrine. A woman first pursued an internal commitment to a public ministry. She had to be convinced of the presence of Christ within and that He spoke through her. She might be uncertain and need support and encouragement from other Friends. When her work as a public exponent of the truth was established she might then believe herself called to carry that truth abroad. In the early years of the Society, these missions were designed to proselytize; later, as the Friends became more withdrawn, they were intended to help keep strong the faith. Of the first 59 publishers of the truth who came to America from 1656 to 1663, nearly half (26) were women; of these, only four were travelling in ministry with their husbands. Many of these women exhibited enormous courage and bravery in the face of the frequently hostile environment and establishments. Mary Dyer may have been unusual in courting death in Massachusetts, but she was not unusual in her determination to spread the Quakers' message. The later ministry, in which women were equally active, could also take them far afield, although they travelled to established meetings to maintain a high level of religious experience. All of these women had the support of their own meetings and were heard with respect at others.

The other area in which Quaker women engaged most actively was the women's meetings, and here we find them playing a part in church governance, the discipline of women, and the control of membership. Some historians have assumed that women's meetings were established to give women enough authority to keep them happy but not enough to make them powerful. The records of women's meetings do convey a sense of lesser bodies, with relatively little money, not given the quasi-judicial function which men's meetings had in dealing with controversy. However, Fox was concerned about the role of women, and his message to them was unconventional; and the Fell women, Margaret and her daughter Sarah, had a great deal to do with the formation of early women's meetings and saw them as an instrument for the expansion of woman's role.

• • •

A notable symbolic act occurred in each meeting as women became accustomed to manage their affairs. The invariably decided to buy a record book (an important investment) and to appoint a clerk. Thereafter, the book was tangible evidence of their activity. Equally important, as Friends began to build permanent meeting houses, women acquired their own space. Typically, meeting houses were built with sliding partitions which could divide them down the center. Women sat on one side, men on the other. During meetings for worship, the partitions were open and all worshiped together, but during meetings for business the partitions would come down, thus providing women and men with separate spaces for the conduct of their separate business.

But the most important function in American meetings, ultimately, was the female share in protection of the institution of marriage, and the maintenance of the unity of membership. Concern that partners be free to marry was important in a mobile group, and particularly in America, an immigrant society. Hence, people who wanted to marry, if they were not native to the meeting in which they expected to wed, had to produce certificates from their prior meetings showing them to be free. It was equally important to know that they were Friends to guarantee the marriage would be "in unity." That is, Friends had to marry Friends, both parties had to demonstrate membership in good standing, and they had to marry in meeting. Marriage out of the meeting, if not repented, led to exclusion from membership for the couple, and perhaps their parents, if they could be shown to have been negligent. This exclusiveness parallels the Puritans' attempt to maintain unity on a larger social scale by keeping dissenters out of the colony; but it prevented domination by either sex in membership in the Friends' meetings.

Women's meetings appointed several members to oversee a marriage. This involved interviews with the couple, not only to examine their intentions, but also to make certain both were convinced Quakers who would keep their family in the Society. Women looked into reputation and even into material considerations. The men's meeting cooperated in this, and the marriage could not take place until the meetings agreed. The women sent representatives to the wedding, to make sure all was done with dignity and decency, according to the Friends' mode. This rigorous protection of marriage in unity was combined with disciplining of men and women who were not regular in meeting attendance. Through these disciplines women's meetings played a role in maintaining a family-based membership in the Society of Friends, one in which neither sex dominated in number, and women retained a share of power.

We can conclude that Quaker women played a more forceful role in the Society of Friends than Puritan women did in the Congregational church. Quaker doctrine provided for a reinterpretation of scriptural prescriptions of female inferiority and submission; Puritans reaffirmed both Genesis and St. Paul. Quaker women, through the Divine Light and their lay ministry, maintained an important position for themselves in the formulation of doctrine; Puritan women were defeated in their attempts to influence doctrine. Quaker women had their own place in church governance, disciplined themselves, and shared control of membership; Puritan women were disciplined to silence, and socialized to accept moral responsibility for the continuation of a Christian community.

The Quakers may have developed an active and workable role for women, but they did not have a major influence on the American Protestant view of women. Never in the mainstream of American religious life, Friends did not retain their dominance in politics or culture even in Pennsylvania, and in the course of the eighteenth century they became more and more introspective, exclusive, and "peculiar." In the face of rigorous discipline numbers decreased, but the religious commitment of those who remained was enhanced. Quaker women, pious and active, may eventually have had some influence on American women as moral custodians; but women of other sects did not learn from the Friends what they needed to know to change their position in the church.

The Puritans, on the other hand, *were* the mainstream of American religious life, and the congregational way, which marked the politics and culture of New England in such distinctive ways, had a far-reaching influence. Friends may have demonstrated the best that the religious revolution of the seventeenth century could do for women; but it was the Puritan mode of female piety and submission to ministerial authority that was to dominate both pew and pulpit in America.

For Further Reading

The Puritan leaders who banished Anne Hutchinson produced the records upon which all subsequent evaluations have been based. Charles Francis Adams published some of the original sources in his *Antinomianism in the Colony of Massachusetts-Bay, 1636-1638* (Boston, 1894). Those same materials, together with other printed and manuscript sources, are collected in David Hall's *The Antinomian Controversy, 1636-1638* (Middletown, 1968). Hall's bibliographical essay identifies additional manuscripts.

The first history of Massachusetts to discuss the dispute was Edward Johnson's *A History of New England* (London, 1654), generally known as *The Wonder-Working Providence of Sion's Saviour in New England*. Johnson adopted the viewpoint common among the opponents of Anne Hutchinson. Cotton Mather's *Magnalia Christi Americana* (London, 1702) likewise treated the Winthrop side sympathetically and the Hutchinsonians as heretics. Anne's great-great-grandson Thomas Hutchinson, governor of Massachusetts and author of a *History of the Colony of Massachusetts Bay* (Boston, 1764), accepted the judgement that her opinions "had like to have produced ruin both to church and state." Most nineteenth century studies, such as John Gorham Palfrey's *History of New England During the Stuart Dynasty* (Boston, 1865), likewise understood the magistrates' need to maintain their authority.

Charles Francis Adams was among the first to reverse the traditional view. Hostile to the premises of Puritan theology, Adams included the Antinomian controversy as one of *Three Episodes of Massachusetts History* (Boston, 1892) in which opponents of the colony's authorities were extolled as champions of liberty and conscience. Subsequent generations of historians followed Adams' lead in depicting Mrs. Hutchinson as a heroine. This trend reached a peak at the time of the three hundredth anniversary of the founding of Massachusetts. Winnifred Rugg's *Unafraid: A Life of Anne Hutchinson* (Boston, 1930), Edith Curtis' *Anne Hutchinson: A Biography* (Cambridge, 1930), and Helen Augur's *An American Jezebel: The Life of Anne Hutchinson* (New York, 1930) all contributed to the myth of Anne Hutchinson as a crusader who battled the narrow-minded bigots of the Bay in the cause of religious freedom.

The 1930s, however, also marked the beginnings of a reevaluation of

New England's Puritan heritage that would contribute to a far more realistic understanding of the Antinomian crisis. The landmark study in this process was Perry Miller's *The New England Mind: The Seventeenth Century* (Cambridge, 1939), which was followed by a second volume, *The New England Mind: From Colony to Province* (Cambridge, 1953). Miller's great accomplishment was in recovering and appreciating Puritan theology. His essay on "'Preparation for Salvation' in Seventeenth Century New England," *Journal of the History of Ideas, 4* (1943), focused on what he saw as the key issue in the Antinomian controversy. In that essay he contended that the orthodox clergy's development of the concept of "preparation" represented a modification of their Calvinist heritage. Although he disagreed with Miller's formulation of the subject, Norman Petit's *The Heart Prepared: Grace and Conversion in Puritan Spiritual Life* (New Haven, 1966) likewise portrays Shepard and the "orthodox" party as the innovators. William K. B. Stoever has challenged that view in the selection contained in this anthology and, more recently, in "*'A Faire and Easie Way to Heaven': Covenant Theology and Antinomianism in Early Massachusetts*" (Middletown, 1978).

James F. Maclear helps both to relate Cotton and Mrs. Hutchinson to their Puritan roots and to explain why many Antinomians became Quakers in "'The Heart of New England Rent': The Mystical Element in Early Puritan History," *Mississippi Valley Historical Review, 42,* (1956). Those who wish to pursue the connections between Puritans, Hutchinsonians, and Quakers should also consult Alan Simpson's *Puritanism in Old and New England* (Chicago, 1955).

Ronald D. Cohen reviews the case against Anne Hutchinson not only in terms of Puritan political ideas but also the particular problems facing the colony at the time in "Church and State in Seventeenth Century Massachusetts: Another Look at the Antinomian Controversy," *Journal of Church and State, 12* (1970), which is reprinted in Alden T. Vaughan and Francis J. Bremer, eds., *Puritan New England: Essays on Religion, Society, and Culture* (New York, 1977). Readers who wish to place the dispute in a broader context should consult Francis J. Bremer's *The Puritan Experiment: New England Society from Bradford to Edwards* (New York 1976) and Edmund S. Morgan's *The Puritan Dilemma, The Story of John Winthrop* (Boston, 1958).

Much still remains to be done in reconstructing the life of women in colonial America. Valuable studies that begin that task are Carol Ruth Berkin, *Within the Conjuror's Circle: Women in Colonial America* (Morristown, 1974); Roger Thompson, *Women in Stuart England and America* (London, 1974); and the relevant sections of Carol Ruth Berkin and Mary Beth Norton, *Women of America: A History* (Boston, 1978). English historians have thus far been more successful than their American counterparts in examining the role of women in Reformed religion. Christopher Hill discusses radical Puritan women in chapter fifteen of *The World Turned Upside Down: Radical Ideas During the English Revolution* (New York,

1972). E. M. Williams' "Women Preachers in the Civil War," *Journal of Modern History*, *I* (0000) and Keith Thomas's "Women and the Civil War Sects," *Past and Present*, *13* (1968) have obvious relevance to those interested in Anne Hutchinson. Material for an interesting comparison between the Massachusetts radical and the outstanding woman of the early Quaker movement can be found in Isobel Ross' biography of *Margaret Fell* (London, 1949).

There are a number of valuable studies of women's conjugal role in Puritan society. Among the best are William and Mary Haller, "The Puritan Art of Love," *Huntington Library Quarterly*, V (1941-42); R. M. Frye, "The Teachings of Classical Puritanism on Conjugal Love," *Studies in the Renaissance*, II (1955); James Johnson, *A Society Ordained by God: English Puritan Marriage Doctrine in the First Half of the Seventeenth Century* (Nashville, 1970); Edmund S. Morgan, *The Puritan Family* (New York, 1966); K. M. Davies, "The Social Condition of Equality—How Original Were Puritan Doctrines of Marriage?", *Social History*, 5 (1977); Keith Thomas, "The Double Standard," *Journal of the History of Ideas*, XX (1959); and Keith Thomas, "The Puritans and Adultry," in Donald Pennington and Keith Thomas, eds., *Puritans and Revolutionaries: Essays Presented to Christopher Hill* (Oxford, 1978).

Stephen Foster's "Puritanism and the Challenge of Heresy, 1630-1660: A Trans-Atlantic Approach", a paper delivered at the 1976 meeting of the Organization of American Historians, explicitly deals with the Anglo-American dimension of the controversy and is virtually alone in asking what "heresy" meant to the Puritans.